FOOD
MYTHS

Nicole Senior

Contents

Introduction

I've always been interested in writing about food myths and have amassed quite a collection over the years both as Nutrition Editor for *Super Food Ideas* magazine and through my regular contributions to *GI News* (http://ginews.blogspot.com). I think it's fun to bust food myths, set the record straight and help people become a bit more relaxed and less stressed about food and eating. I guess if I could summarise my approach it would be: commonsense backed up by evidence. I also see this as a great opportunity to fly the flag for evidence-based nutrition and dietitian-nutritionists: we are highly trained specialists on food for health. But there is a more serious side to the subject.

Food myths are prevalent in societies where food is abundant and choices are practically endless. In stark and distressing contrast, people in poor countries struggle to get enough food to survive. Are we fussy with our diets and vulnerable to food myths because we're too well fed? By following fad diets, are we desperately clutching at ideas to narrow down our food options because they are now overwhelming? Are we looking to fix our broader unease with our hectic modern lifestyles? Has our food supply become so far removed from its source that we are reacting against it?

These are deep questions that deserve another book all on their own but I'd ask you to consider them when understanding why food myths persist. A bit of perspective is always good.

I hope this book achieves peace of mind for you, and above all a renewed appreciation, respect and enjoyment of good food. After all, nothing should get in the way of the love of food and sharing it with the people we care about.

> If more of us valued food and cheer and song above hoarded gold, it would be a merrier world.
>
> —J.R.R. Tolkien

Declaration of interest: I provide nutrition consultancy services to food and communications companies as well as the media, health and community organisations. For more information go to www.nicolesenior.com.au.

Reading about nutrition

I write about food myths and never seem to run out of topics. Opinions and beliefs about food are commonplace; however, nutrition recommendations from reputable sources are distilled over time through a rigorous process of assessing scientific evidence, not opinions or anecdotes. And it's not just well-meaning friends, health food store employees, neighbours and websites you need to worry about.

The media often get it wrong. Or at least they misconstrue the message or over-simplify it. Journalists love a catchy headline. As a result readers can get the wrong idea. For example, 'Drink Amazon jungle juice and lose weight'. Here's how that all gets out of context. In nutrition research terms, a study that finds an association between eating a food or nutrient (say, Amazon jungle juice) and a health indicator (say, weight loss) in a particular group (say, Amazonian Indians) does not mean Amazon jungle juice will help **you** lose weight.

An epidemiological or population study (of populations and their health status) like this cannot prove or disprove causation—it merely identifies an association that needs further research. This kind of study is also prone to methodological problems such as: did they have enough Amazonian Indians in the study to ensure the results are valid? (A certain number of people are needed otherwise it may be impossible to draw worthwhile conclusions from the results.) How was the indigenous subjects' intake of Amazonian jungle juice assessed? Did it rely on their memory of past consumption? (Memories fade.) Were the right questions and/or research methods used in this unusual group? (Do Amazonian Indians even think about food in a quantitative way?) Was their level of physically activity properly factored in? (Being very active would also cause weight loss.) Additional research to further demonstrate a causative link might include: basic science about the mechanism of action (how could the jungle juice actually work?), and—ideally—intervention studies in which people are given jungle juice in controlled conditions to see what happens.

The gold-standard intervention study is a double-blind, randomised, placebo-controlled trial—often referred to as a **randomised controlled study**—in which the research subjects are divided into groups, and given either the drug (or food, or task) being trialled or a placebo that appears to be similar to what is being tested. Both the subjects and researchers have no idea which group received what (jungle juice or a placebo), and whether the intervention (what is being tested) works statistically better than a placebo. It's only later that the researchers are told which group is which. Not just one of these randomised controlled studies is needed, but it needs to be repeated many times to ensure the results are robust and repeatable.

Alas, often these issues are not considered by journalists working on the basis of a press release for one study, racing toward deadline, and who most often have no scientific background.

I use an evidence-based approach. This means I rely on published studies that have been peer-reviewed: that is, other research experts have gone over the paper before it is published to make sure it is of a high standard. I give most weight to the highest level studies—randomised controlled trials. I cite lower level population studies to remind readers of support for an important dietary principle; however, I do this when I know there are many studies that also agree with it—journalists usually do not have this knowledge. I also rely on health organisations with scientific experts to assess the evidence for me—for example, the American Heart Association, the National Health and Medical Research Council, the Heart Foundation, and the UK Cochrane Database, which publish evidence-based reviews on a range of topics with references. I also trust *NHS Choices* 'Behind the Headlines' and the Harvard University School of Public Health to review the evidence behind nutrition in the news.

I sometimes receive feedback from readers of my books and articles urging me to read a book or magazine in order to educate myself about an alternative view, but their suggestions often aren't trustworthy sources of information. After all, books and magazines vary widely in how well they are researched, how much scientific evidence they use and how well they have assessed the scientific studies. No qualifications are required to publish a book or a magazine article—anyone can do it if they have a marketable concept. Authors vary wildly in their credentials and experience too.

The best nutrition books and magazines are those written by suitably trained experts on the topic, using scientifically sound research and evidence-based content. In my experience these are nutrition academics and dietitian-nutritionists. Much like you wouldn't ask your butcher to cut your hair, I wouldn't buy a book on nutrition written by a non-dietitian or non-nutritionist. I would buy one by a dietitian-nutritionist who is accredited by a national body such as the British Dietetic Association, American Dietetic Association, Dietitians Association of Australia, New Zealand Dietetic Association and Dietitians of Canada. Saying a medical doctor is close enough to a dietitian-nutritionist is like saying a butcher is close enough to a hairdresser because they both use sharp instruments. Close, but not close enough!

KEY INFO Nutrition science is specialised, complex and evolving. Many people get it wrong.

LONG STORY SHORT Misinformation, misunderstanding and conspiracy theories abound about food, nutrition and health. Don't believe everything you read or hear—maintain a critical eye to sort the wheat from the chaff and only trust the true experts.

HUNGRY FOR MORE? Accredited/registered dietitians in the UK, USA, Canada, New Zealand and Australia are university-trained specialists in nutrition. They are the best equipped health professionals to help you with diet and health.

PART 1

Diets and weight loss

I've often wondered why bad 'diets' seem to do so well. How can a diet that doesn't work be so popular? How can a product that is unsubstantiated become a bestseller? It's a tribute to good marketing but it also indicates the number of people struggling with excess weight, and the lengths they will go to in order to get lose it.

Unfortunately for many, the 'moderation' message is boring and unappealing: instead, it seems as if we need to be shaken out of our old ways and shocked into submission. Perhaps moderation is far too sensible and we have a craving for risk? Perhaps we are just too impatient? Perhaps we latch on to the first person or company who seems to understand our difficulties? Who knows? The situation isn't helped by the diet industry, which knows the moderation message doesn't sell. It comes up with all manner of trumped-up benefits and half-baked theories about why their diets will actually work when all they are doing is selling creative ways to eat fewer kilojoules.

To lose weight we must reconcile the—boring—fact that we must eat less and exercise more, with ensuring we eat quality foods to meet our nutritional needs ... and eat foods we like ... and be able to afford them ... and please all the family ... and prepare food quickly. You can appreciate the challenges.

Blacklisting particular nutrients such as carbs or fats, like many fad diets do, is not helpful. What we should be doing is prioritising nutrient-rich foods from all the food groups in suitable amounts according to how much energy we need. This is not easy, and therefore quick fixes have the allure of a cold drink after a walk in the desert.

It's a pity there are so many myths about weight loss and dieting to choose from (I couldn't fit them all in). It's also a great shame that so many people have wasted so much money and experienced so much heartache and disappointment at the hands of myth-spinners. I say: don't get mad or get even—get savvy instead. Read on and you could save yourself a lot of money and grief.

⊙ You should eat according to your blood type

There is an attraction to a diet that claims we all fall into distinct 'types' which each require a specific dietary approach. It just seems to make sense. But just because it sounds plausible doesn't mean it is. There is no scientific foundation to eating according to your blood type, despite the fact that a doctor is peddling the diet.

Genetic variation between individuals is the reason why some people don't do as well on certain diets, and why some people don't respond in the same way to dietary change in scientific studies. This has been known for decades and started the new scientific frontier of nutrigenetics: designing diets and eating plans according to your genetic make-up. Geneticists who work in nutrigenetics say the blood-type diet is silly: it's the equivalent of reading tea leaves to determine what to have for dinner. This is because there are hundreds of known polymorphisms (genetic variations) that influence diet and health, and none of them relates to blood type. For example, there are polymorphisms (variants) that affect how your LDL or 'bad' cholesterol responds to eating fat; others affect how homocysteine levels respond to a vegetarian diet lower in vitamin B12.

Austrian Karl Landsteiner discovered blood types in 1901 and this allowed the first safe blood transfusions. He received a Nobel prize for his work in 1930. Blood types A, B, AB and O are distinguished by the different combinations of antigens on the surface of the red blood cells and antibodies in the plasma. For example, blood type A has A antigens on the surface of the red blood cells and B antibodies in the plasma. Somebody with blood group B has B antigens on the surface of their red blood cells and A antibodies in their blood plasma. If you receive the wrong blood type as a transfusion, antigens on the surface of the donor red blood cells will react with the antibodies in your plasma and clump together, impairing circulation, and may even kill you.

How blood type relates to the food you should eat is where the creativity comes in: proponents of blood-type diets say blood type also correlates with a number of characteristics affecting digestion—for example, type O produces more stomach acid and therefore can more easily digest meat, and type As should be vegetarian because they produce less acid. Even if type Os did produce a bit more acid—and this is a very big 'if'—it would make negligible difference to their ability to digest meat. Although acid is a big help, it is protein-digesting enzymes from the pancreas that do all the heavy lifting when it comes to protein digestion. Millions of people take medications to significantly reduce acid production because of acid reflux, yet they can still digest meat.

KEY INFO Your blood group has nothing to do with your ability to digest food, or what diet best suits you. There are hundreds of known genetic variants that do affect diet and health and none of them relate to blood type. The serious study of individualising diets according to genetic makeup is called nutrigenetics.

LONG STORY SHORT The blood-type diet does not enjoy the backing of good scientific evidence but despite this it has made the bestseller list—go figure.

HUNGRY FOR MORE? Type 'nutrigenetics' into your favourite search engine (but talk with your doctor before embarking on any genetic testing).

⊙ Food combining helps you lose weight

There are several fad diets that promote 'food combining'—or not eating certain foods together. They advocate this way of eating for wellness and weight loss. They promote avoiding the consumption of proteins and carbohydrate foods together (such as meat and pasta, or egg on toast), and eating only fruit until midday. They say that certain foods digest at different rates and can interfere with one another, and that fruit should never be eaten with other foods because proteins and fats take too long to digest, causing fruit to 'ferment' in the stomach (see *Meat takes weeks to digest*, page 140). How this relates to weight I'll never know!

Some bad food combos to avoid

- Don't sprinkle unprocessed bran on everything because bran contains phytates which bind to minerals such as iron and zinc and reduce their absorption.

- Don't overdo caffeine because it can interfere with calcium balance and impair bone health. Enjoy caffeinate containing foods and drinks in moderation.

- Go easy on the salt as more sodium in the diet increases the body's need for calcium. Skip added salt and buy salt-reduced products.

- Don't drink tea with meals because the tannins reduce the absorption of iron from plant foods such as breads and cereal—enjoy your tea between meals.

If you follow this diet, you end up eating less (and thus lose weight) but it has nothing to do with food combining. It's more to do with the number of meals and dishes that are off limits because they break the rules. There is no scientific basis for such strict food combining. The body is designed to digest a variety of foods and nutrients in many different combinations. In fact when our gut is at its most immature during infancy, Mother Nature's perfect food—breast milk—is a nutritionally complete mixture of carbs, fats and protein. Legumes are some of the healthiest foods around and they are a combination of protein and slow-release carbohydrates. Food combining makes no sense and has not been practised by any traditional societies in human history.

True, there are some foods and drinks that are better off not eaten together (see page 19), but these combinations bear no relation to the advice in fad diet books and have nothing to do with weight loss.

KEY INFO The body is absolutely capable of digesting all kinds of wild and wonderful food combinations.

LONG STORY SHORT Food-combining diets are unscientific.

HUNGRY FOR MORE? Don't bother.

▶ You can eat as much fruit as you want

If I had a dollar for every person who said, 'I only eat healthy foods but I'm still fat', I'd be sailing the world in my own fully staffed yacht! Although eating only healthy foods will give you a head start, you can still eat too much and gain weight.

Fruit is one of those foods with a well-earned health halo (positively angelic)—however, it is not a 'free' food because fruit still contains kilojoules. All the fibre, vitamins, minerals and phytochemicals fruit contain do not cancel out the kilojoules. An all-fruit diet is a bad idea because you can't get all the nutrition you need from fruit (despite the claims of 'fruitarians') and because you could still end up eating too many kilojoules to lose weight. If you're watching your kilojoule intake you also need to watch how much fruit you eat and limit it to two pieces a day (and perhaps three if you are very active or bigger). Fresh fruit is better than juice because of its fibre and filling power.

What is a serve of fruit?
IT'S ABOUT THE AMOUNT THAT FITS IN YOUR HAND ...

- 1 medium piece of fruit, such as an apple, pear, peach or orange

- 1 cup of fruit pieces, such as sliced strawberries or melon

- 2 small pieces of fruit, such as plums or apricots.

Fruit juices are seen as the healthier alternative but although they have the advantage of providing vitamin C and antioxidants, they have as much sugar and kilojoules as soft drink! Juice bars are popular but the serving sizes can be very large, containing the juice from as many as five or six pieces of fruit but none of the beneficial fibre. Try diluting small amounts of juice (½ cup) with water to tone down the sweetness and energy content while maximising refreshment.

Dried fruit is rich in fibre and nutrients; however, it is a concentrated form of fruit that packs quite a kilojoule punch. Trekkers and mountaineers eat 'trail mix' with dried fruit because it has a lot of energy in a small amount of food. Unless you're trekking or doing hard labour, it's best to keep dried fruit to a minimum.

KEY INFO Fruit is healthy but it is not kilojoule-free. Fruit juice has as much sugar and just as many kilojoules as soft drink. Dried fruit is very high in kilojoules too.

LONG STORY SHORT Stick to fresh fruit rather than juice to get the beneficial fibre and limit kilojoules. For most people two pieces of fruit a day is enough. Limit dried fruit to small amounts occasionally.

HUNGRY FOR MORE? Check out the energy content of fruit and fruit products at www.calorieking.com; www.caloriecounting. co.uk or www.calorieking.com.au.

▶ You need to eat every few hours to lose weight

I've read many websites, books and diet programs that say you must eat every few hours or the body will go into 'starvation mode', which slows the metabolism, impedes weight loss and encourages weight regain. This is incorrect. I'm all for eating regular balanced meals, but insisting everyone snack every few hours is simply not necessary and may actually encourage overeating and weight gain.

When it comes to weight loss, the total amount of food you eat is what matters—not how often you eat. I'm not recommending it, but you could eat one large meal a day and still lose weight if the energy contained in the meal was less than you needed.

Individuals vary in their need to snack, and this can change over a lifetime. I remember as a young adult experiencing quite debilitating hunger (I called it cottonwool head) if I didn't eat between meals, yet now I find I don't need to. If I feel peckish between meals the reason is often boredom or because food is there, not because I'm actually hungry. Does this sound familiar?

The practical downside of the 'you must snack' advice is that it's hard to find suitable snacks. The snacks that are easily available are usually nutrient-poor and oversized. Our demand for convenience means it is too easy to snack badly.

To lose weight you need to eat less and move more. If you perform better having snacks between meals, make sure they are nutritious foods and fit within your daily kilojoule budget (see *I can't lose weight because I have a slow metabolism*, page 41)—you may need to reduce the size of your meals to achieve this. If you don't need to snack between meals, don't.

People with diabetes, however, are better off spreading their carbs evenly over the day to manage blood glucose levels. This is because their hormone insulin doesn't work very well and their bodies struggle to process large quantities of food containing carbohydrates at the one time. Eating 'little and often' is easier to handle.

KEY INFO When it comes to weight loss, the total amount of food you eat is what matters, not how often you eat.

LONG STORY SHORT Eating too often may hinder your weight loss efforts. Only snack if you're hungry and snacking doesn't push you into over-eating.

HUNGRY FOR MORE? See *I can't lose weight because I have a slow metabolism*, page 41.

⊙ Avoid carbs after 5PM to lose weight

Avoiding carbs after 5PM is popular advice, often given by people in the fitness industry to assist their clients lose weight. There's even a diet book of the same name. Following this advice might even work in the short term. But the timing of carb intake is physiologically irrelevant—it's the amount you eat that's important. There's not a single study on the US Library of Medicine (PubMed) database about carbohydrate timing and weight loss (but there's plenty on carb timing and athletic performance, if you're interested).

The US Library of Medicine, or PubMed, is a database of published scientific articles (mostly abstracts or summaries but sometimes the whole article) on all aspects of health and medicine, including articles on diet and nutrition. This tool is used by professionals—you can search for articles too at www. ncbi.nlm.nih.gov/pubmed/.

Like other diets that restrict a particular nutrient or food group, the advice to avoid carbs after 5PM is simply a kilojoule reduction strategy dressed up as something catchier. When you think of a typical evening meal of chicken, noodles and vegetables, it's not hard to see how skipping noodles creates a kilojoule deficit. If you can do it, great—it is possible to eat enough grain foods (preferably wholegrain and low GI) at other times during the day. However, a common experience of evening carb avoiders is they are still hungry after dinner and that's when TV snacking can wreak havoc. Biscuits, chocolate and sweets are common night-time saboteurs and they all contain carbohydrates. (And a side note: many people don't understand that sugar is a carbohydrate, which results in starchy foods getting a bad rap and sugar sailing through unsullied.) Unfortunately, the biscuits and chocolate also contain hefty amounts of saturated fat and kilojoules. This carb-craving may be physiological or psychological but it doesn't really matter—the kilojoule damage is done.

The 'no carbs after 5PM' rule—and its variants 3PM, 4PM and 6PM—is part of a dieting mentality we know is inherently unsustainable, although to be fair it is a much more moderate version of a low-carb diet. By deliberately depriving ourselves of commonly eaten, enjoyable, satisfying foods we build up psychological pressure that eventually results in overeating blow-outs: the classic dieting merry-go-round.

KEY INFO The time you eat carbs makes no difference to your weight—it's the total amount you eat over the day that counts. Withholding carbs at the evening meal can trigger late-night snacking.

LONG STORY SHORT Eat smaller portions of carb-rich core foods such as bread, pasta, rice, noodles and the like, and choose lower GI versions combined with plenty of vegetables, satisfying amounts of milk products and lean meat, chicken, fish or vegetarian alternatives.

HUNGRY FOR MORE? Refer to www.hsph.harvard.edu/nutritionsource/what-should-you-eat/carbohydrates-full-story.

⊙ Obesity is a failure of personal responsibility

'Just say no' used to be the catch-cry of conservative anti-drug campaigners and now it is used against the obese as well. Parents are blamed for their fat children, and fat adults are criticised for their gluttony and sloth. Just as prohibition and criminalisation do not reduce drug use, blaming the individual does nothing to stop the obesity epidemic. To use an old mine safety analogy, it's like blaming the canary for dropping dead in its cage rather than the noxious gases that killed it.

Of course personal responsibility plays a role and education is important. However, if our entire environment and way of life is fattening, only the strong can and do resist. This is where we're at: we live in an obesogenic (obesity-causing) world. Our jobs are less active, our cities are built for cars not people and we're surrounded by labour-saving devices so we can spend more time sitting in front of computer and TV screens. We have become victims of our own success.

The gluttony and sloth argument also falls down when you consider the speed at which the epidemic has taken hold: we can't all have developed serious character flaws so quickly. The speed of the epidemic suggests something about our world has changed, not us.

Obesity is the result of many complex factors over which the obese person has little control. In developed countries, it is the socially disadvantaged who experience the worst health, including obesity. A more socially equal society would reduce obesity rates, but governments are reticent to do this. Wealth trumps health every time. Our whole food system is designed to produce food as cheaply as possible with no regard to nutritional content and health effects (or environmental sustainability); thus we have a food supply full of highly processed, energy-dense, nutrient-poor foods. And they are sold in overly large portions.

Eating well takes effort and skills and in this day and age of longer working hours and more women in the workforce, we're short on both. It's little wonder we're increasingly outsourcing our food, and unfortunate that so much of the food we buy is fattening and unhealthy: exhibit A—fast food. Eating well costs more and this will only get worse as food prices rise, as is expected as environmental degradation and climate change start to bite and the global population balloons.

Removing the onus on the individual and creating healthier, less fattening environments is the way forward. We need to make healthy choices easy choices.

KEY INFO The obesity epidemic is driven by dramatic changes to our environment and lifestyle, as well as social and economic factors. Blaming individuals is not effective, further entrenches social disadvantage and exacerbates human misery (no one wants to be obese).

LONG STORY SHORT Although education is important to help individuals make informed food choices, we need to fix the environment to make it less fattening and more supportive of healthy choices.

HUNGRY FOR MORE? Read *The World is Fat* by Barry Popkin; *Planet Obesity* by Garry Egger and Boyd Swinburn; and Dr Linda Bacon's Health At Every Size website at www.haescommunity. org/.

⊙ Some foods have negative calories

We've all heard the stories about celery taking more energy to digest than it actually contains, but is this true? Moreover, would the concept of negative calories in some foods make any difference in the quest for healthy weight loss? My answer is 'no' to the first, but 'maybe' to the second.

If thinking whole fresh foods such as vegetables contain negative kilojoules helps you to eat more of them, go ahead. The [health benefit of the] end certainly justifies the [mistaken] means. But if the overweight and vulnerable rely on a crazy unbalanced diet featuring larges amounts of these foods to the exclusion of most others, then this myth should be nipped in the bud.

Although celery does not take more kilojoules to digest than it contains, it is naturally low in kilojoules—a helpful characteristic of most vegetables and the reason why sensible weight loss diets emphasise eating plenty of them (not to mention their grocery list of other health benefits). Of course, their low-kilojoule status is compromised by eating them with peanut butter or cream cheese (is there any other vegetable that lends itself better to filling up the middle with something tasty?). Let's be honest: celery doesn't taste that great on its own. Lower kilojoule options to 'fill the gap' are tomato salsa or hummus (chickpea dip). My favourite way to enjoy celery is sliced in a stir-fry with lots of other vegetable friends and some lean chicken, beef, pork or tofu, nestled on a bed of brown rice or noodles.

At the heart of many nutrition myths is a kernel of truth, and in this case it is the notion that whole foods rather than overly processed foods take more digestive effort, and in some cases hold back a little of their energy because it's too hard for the body to liberate. The extra digestive effort starts in the mouth—some foods need a lot more chewing. This is very positive because of the energy it requires, the way it slows down eating to allow the brain to register satiety (fullness), and of course the direct effect on strengthening the jaw muscles and massaging the teeth and gums. The hard and complex structure of some foods such as wholegrains, nuts and legumes actually prevent all their nutrients (and kilojoules) from being fully released during digestion, and some simply pass straight through. This could be a reason why high-fibre diets help with weight loss and why nuts aren't as fattening as you'd expect. Conversely, many processed foods are easy to overeat because they go down so easily. Think of fluffy white bread, doughnuts, cupcakes, mashed potato, ice-cream and even juice. In the case of fluffy white bread and mashed potato, these low-digestive-effort foods have a high GI (see page 46). For many reasons, it's worth working harder for your food.

Reality check

Whenever you encounter a diet that advocates something as simple as eating celery (or whatever) will help you lose weight, ask yourself the following reality-check questions (and you can insert any other food in place of celery):

- Do I like eating lots of celery?
- How long can I keep eating lots of celery?
- Will eating lots of celery make me feel deprived?
- Will eating lots of celery help me feel good about myself?
- Will eating celery prevent me from over-eating other high-kilojoule foods?
- Can I eat lots of celery and still enjoy social eating with family and friends?
- Will eating lots of celery encourage me to be more physically active?

Key info It is impossible for a food to require more energy to digest than it contains.

Long story short Celery is low in kilojoules but you don't use more kilojoules than it contains to digest it. But even if you did, when you eat other foods with it (like cream cheese!) it cancels out any benefits anyway. It's a good idea to eat plenty of minimally processed plant foods such as legumes, wholegrains and nuts because they can help keep your weight down.

Hungry for more? Crunch on a stick of celery as you check out Jo Rogers' fabulous book, *What Food is That? & How Healthy is It?*; George Mateljan's *The World's Healthiest Foods*; and www.whfoods.com.

⊙ Vegetarian diets are healthier

Heart Food, a book I wrote with Veronica Cuskelly, has a picture of a mouth-watering steak on the front cover. A couple of people expressed surprise at this choice, and couldn't believe that meat was healthy. Of course a balanced diet including lean meat can be healthy and heart friendly, but meat often gets a bum rap—much of it deserved because our portions are too large and our meat choices too fatty. But is going meat-free the true path to wellness? Well, a vegetarian diet can have a few holes in it too and lack key nutrients such as iron, zinc, B12 and omega-3 DHA. Here are a few myths about vegetarianism.

Vegetarians live longer

While it's true that the Seventh Day Adventist vegetarian community in Loma Linda, California, are one of the most long-lived in the world, under the cold light of science this can't be fully explained by their diet. The people in this community also don't drink alcohol, are physically active, and have strong religious faith and social connectedness. Elsewhere in the world there are equally long-lived communities that do include animal foods in their diet, such as in the Nicoya Peninsula of Costa Rica, Sardinia in Italy and Okinawa in Japan—interestingly, although they do eat meat, their diets are based on plant foods (as are heart-healthy diets today). The take-home message is, if you eat meat make sure you eat plenty of vegetables, do lots of exercise and pray!

Vegetarian dishes in restaurants are healthier options

In my experience, this is the exception rather than the rule. Unfortunately, vegetarian dishes tend to be heavy on cheese, cream and pastry (for example, quiche or nachos), and thus heavy on kilojoules and artery-clogging saturated fat and salt. Unless the chef is clued up on vegetarian cuisine, you end up with a meat-free version of an existing dish (such as vegetable pasta) rather than a well-balanced meal with suitable meat alternatives such as legumes and nuts. Teen girls please note: throwing the meat out of your burger does not make it a vegetarian meal! The best option is to research a restaurant guidebook, or the web if you're looking for suitable vegan dishes (containing no animal products at all). More education about healthy meat-free meals is sorely needed.

There is enough iron in plant foods

I saw a bumper sticker on the back of a cattle truck that said, 'seven days without meat makes one weak'. Very clever, but is there any truth to it? Maybe, when you consider plant foods such as wholegrains, legumes and nuts contain non-haem (or non-heme) iron of which only 5 per cent is absorbed. Added to this, vegetarian diets contain very high levels of phytates and oxalates which inhibit iron absorption. Eating foods rich in vitamin C can enhance the absorption of non-haem iron, but never reaches the bioavailability of haem iron. The haem iron in meat, chicken, pork and fish is absorbed much better: between 15 and 35 per cent, and in a mixed meal the haem iron enhances the non-haem iron absorption as well. Many vegetarians do fine without meat because their iron needs are lower, but children, teenagers, pregnant women and athletes need more and risk going short. Low iron can cause poor energy levels, fatigue and poor immunity, and delayed cognitive development in children.

Sure, meat-lovers would do well to take a leaf out of the vegetarian book by including more protective plant foods, but vegetarian diets have their hazards as well. The take-out message is that avowed carnivores and vegans are dietary extremes, whereas health is so often found in the happy medium. *Vive l'omnivore!*

KEY INFO Although they contain plenty of protective plant foods, vegetarian diets can lack essential nutrients such as iron, zinc, vitamin B12 and omega-3 DHA.

LONG STORY SHORT There's no need to banish meat to enjoy a healthy diet. Eat meat lean and in modest portions in a plant food based diet, and make sure you get some exercise and have strong social connections for wellbeing.

HUNGRY FOR MORE? See *Meat is fattening*, page 136; *Spinach is a good source of iron*, page 223; and www. bluezones.com about the world's longest lived peoples.

⊙ A low-fat diet is best for weight loss

The most famous fall guy for the obesity epidemic is dietary fat and we are still living with the legacy of the 'low-fat' mantra. Just look at the abundance of 'low-fat' and 'light' foods in supermarkets. Yet at the very same time this low-fat revolution was taking place, the levels of overweight and obesity increased.

Weight loss is the result of eating less kilojoules and exercising more. The trick is to maintain a high nutrient intake in fewer kilojoules—this is where food choice is paramount. Choosing the most nutrient-dense foods from all of the food groups will ensure you stay well-nourished at the same time as burning body fat. A fat-free diet does not contain enough essential fatty acids and fat-soluble vitamins, and it also leaves a massive flavour black hole. A Cochrane Review (the ants' pants and bees' knees of scientific studies) of research concluded there is no advantage to low-fat diets over kilojoule-restricted diets for weight loss. You can still lose weight eating healthy fats so long as your diet is kilojoule-controlled (and it will taste a lot better too). A healthy diet contains around 30 per cent of kilojoules as fat, which in an average diet of 8700kJ (2080 calories) is around 70g (2½oz) a day, or down to around 50g (1¾oz) a day for someone on a weight-loss diet. These fats should come from unsaturated sources such as oils and margarine spreads, as well as the healthy fats naturally present in foods like nuts, seeds, oily fish and avocado.

Just because a food is low in fat doesn't mean it is low in kilojoules. Foods with a low moisture content such as 'baked not fried' or 'light' biscuits, crackers and crisps are great examples of foods that are still high in kilojoules despite being made to a lower fat recipe. They are also extremely easy to overeat.

There is a place for low-fat foods—in the dairy aisle. Because dairy foods are a major source of artery-clogging saturated fat, low-fat versions of these nutrient-rich foods are a change for the better and recommended for everyone, including children from two years of age. Low-fat dairy foods such as milk and yoghurt contain just as much calcium and are also satisfying and low GI (see page 46), making them a heart-friendly food.

KEY INFO Some fat is essential for health and wellbeing—fat-free diets are unhealthy. Fats also add flavour and enjoyment to food. It is recommended that around 30 per cent of your daily kilojoules come from fat, which is about 70g (2½oz) a day on average.

LONG STORY SHORT To lose weight you need to eat fewer kilojoules, not avoid fat altogether. Even on a weight-loss diet you need around 50g (1¾oz) fats a day.

HUNGRY FOR MORE? Check out your daily intakes of nutrients at www.cnpp.usda.gov/DGAs2010-PolicyDocument.htm; http://gda.ciaa.eu/asp2/guideline-daily-amounts.asp; www.gdalabel.org.uk; or www.mydailyintake.net.au.

The Cochrane Collaboration

Established in 1993, this is an international network of more than 28,000 dedicated people from over 100 countries. They work together to help health-care providers, policy-makers, patients, their advocates and carers make well-informed decisions about health care, based on the best available research evidence.

They do this by comparing and analysing all the research done in specific areas and publishing their results in the Cochrane Reviews—over 4600 so far—which are available online in The Cochrane Library. Their work is internationally recognised as the benchmark for high-quality information about the effectiveness of health care. See www.cochrane.org.

⊙ Thin people are healthier

How many times have you thought or heard, 'she [or he] is thin so she can eat anything and doesn't have to worry'? It's almost as if the slender folk among us appear untouched by the afflictions of fatties. But being slight of frame is no longer a guarantee all is well on the inside—where it really counts. British Professor Jimmy Bell coined these folk 'TOFIs': Thin Outside, Fat Inside.

The advent of sophisticated medical imaging machines means we can now look at where fat is stored in the body. Apparently thin people can still carry risky amounts of fat around their internal organs (visceral fat). A US study by the Mayo Clinic, which measured 6000 adults over a period of nine years, found 20 to 30 per cent of people fell into this thin-but-fat category. Even though they don't look overweight, people with 'metabolic obesity' are at greater risk of all the usual diseases we associate with fatness, including high cholesterol, heart disease, high blood pressure, stroke and diabetes.

So how do you know if you're metabolically obese? Apart from the use of expensive imaging equipment, the easiest thing to do is to measure your waist.

	INCREASED RISK Greater than …	GREATLY INCREASED RISK Greater than …
Men	94cm (37 inches)	102cm (40 inches)
Women	80cm (31½ inches)	94cm (37 inches)

The good news is that visceral fat is the easiest to move by eating less and moving more. It's your body's easy access storage depot of spare fuel. Avoiding this kind of fat may also depend on the type of food you eat. An analysis of almost 49,000 Europeans participating in the European Prospective Investigation into Cancer and Nutrition (EPIC) study found higher energy density (more kilojoules per gram) and higher glycemic index (GI) diets were associated with visceral fatness. Enjoying low GI foods can help. And on the flipside, if you are larger it doesn't mean you are—or have to be—unhealthy. Eating the right foods and exercising regularly can balance the health ledger in your favour.

KEY INFO Thin people can still carry fat around their organs and this places them at increased risk of chronic disease. There's now a new name for this thin and fat state: 'metabolically obese.'

LONG STORY SHORT Just because you look thin or have skinny legs doesn't mean you're healthy on the inside. Measure your waist to find out if you have too much fat on the inside.

HUNGRY FOR MORE? Enter 'ethnic specific waist measure targets' into your search engine.

Is there just one waist measure target for everyone?

Certain regional and/or ethnic groups have a higher risk of disease at a lower BMI (a measure of body mass) because they have a predisposition for storing visceral fat: people from south-east Asia and India are considered overweight at a BMI of 23 rather than 25 for the general population. South-east Asian and Indian men—typically with skinny legs and a pot belly—have increased risk at a waist measurement of 90cm (35½ inches).

⊙ Detox diets are good for you

Detox diets never seem to go out of fashion with the super health-conscious. They are a boon for purveyors of books, powders and potions. Everything from weight gain, tiredness and poor concentration have been attributed to dreaded 'toxins' invading us from within. However, before you shun everything delicious and subsist on liquid tonics for days or weeks on end (along with a little purging colonic irrigation), you should know that much of the noise around detoxing is hype. In fact, detoxing may well be bad for you—and make you fat!

The marketers of expensive detox products fail to mention that your liver performs this function for free. Although it's true that the liver doesn't take too kindly to abuses such as obesity, excessive alcohol and a junk-food diet, it does not require the extremes promoted by detox diets to keep it happy and healthy. Caffeine, dairy food, wheat, sugar and red meat are commonly forbidden on detox regimes, yet they are not inherently toxic or harmful. Quite the contrary: dairy food and (lean) red meat provide essential nutrients necessary for a healthy and well balanced diet. It's a good idea to enjoy caffeinated drinks and sugar in moderation, but there's no reason to avoid them altogether.

Alcohol is toxic and is one of the few things detox programs are correct in suggesting you avoid to give your body a break. Luckily, our liver shines again in its ability to naturally detoxify alcohol by burning it for fuel: very rich fuel that can and will make you fat if you overindulge. The down side is the liver will become diseased and break down if you drink too much alcohol (unless you kill yourself through misadventure first). Go easy and all will be well.

Many detox diet regimes promote rapid weight loss, and this may be harmful in more ways than just feeling hungry and deprived. Many industrial pollutants (such as organochlorines) are stored in body fat and released back into the body during rapid weight loss. Ironically, emerging theories suggest these chemicals may tip the metabolic balance against fat-burning, and may cause weight re-gain.

Detox diets make you think you have to do something drastic to look after yourself—this simply isn't necessary or sustainable. If you've over-indulged: eat lighter, stay off the booze and be more active. Healthy living is not an extreme sport—it is within your reach.

KEY INFO Weight gain is not caused by toxins. The liver is the body's de-toxifier.

LONG STORY SHORT You do not have to stop eating core foods such as meat and dairy and live on liquids to detoxify the body (see *Meat myths*, pages 125–43, and *Milk myths*, pages 106–24). Drinking less alcohol will reduce the toxic load.

HUNGRY FOR MORE? Enter 'dangers of detox' into your search engine

⊙ I can't lose weight because I have a slow metabolism

Many people believe they have difficulty losing weight because they have a 'slow metabolism', implying that this is outside their control. This isn't true. (An exception is poor thyroid function, which slows metabolism and requires treatment with medication.) Boosting your own metabolism is possible, but perhaps not in the ways you think. You can increase your metabolic rate by gaining muscle, eating more and increasing the amount of exercise you do.

What is metabolism?

The term 'metabolism' (or metabolic rate) refers to the amount of energy the body uses each day—like a daily energy budget—and is measured as kilojoules/calories. Spending more energy than your daily budget means you need to dip into your energy savings: body fat. Unlike a financial deficit, an energy deficit can be a good thing because you lose weight. Metabolism consists of three basic components: Basal Metabolic Rate (BMR); thermogenesis, and physical activity. There are ways you can boost spending on all three fronts.

Basic Metabolic Rate is the energy you spend to sustain basic physiological processes such as keeping your heart beating, your brain and nervous system firing and your liver and kidneys working. Your BMR is primarily related to your lean body mass, so developing and maintaining muscle is a great way to spend more energy (even when you're sitting still). There's no need to sign up for Mr/Ms Universe, but ensuring you do some resistance (strength) training as part of your fitness regime is recommended. Remember not all resistance training is lifting dumbbells in a gym—you can also use your own body weight such as doing lunges, squats and push-ups, or using therabands (large rubber bands used for resistance exercises). Many yoga and pilates exercises build muscle strength as well as flexibility.

Talk to a fitness professional about a suitable resistance training program for you.

Thermogenesis is the energy you spend to digest and metabolise your food. Starving yourself actually lowers your energy budget as well as having the obvious negative physical and psychological consequences. Interestingly, protein needs more energy to utilise and this is one of the reasons higher protein diets seem to work. Ensure you eat enough food at regular intervals and include protein foods such as lean meat, skinless chicken, fish, eggs, dairy food, legumes and nuts in your meals and snacks. Don't go to extremes with the protein and squeeze out smart carbs such as wholegrains, fruits and legumes, but simply balance your meals with some protein foods. For example, rather than just a salad sandwich on wholegrain bread, 'beef' things up a little by adding some lean meat, chicken, salmon, tofu or cottage cheese.

Physical activity is perhaps the most obvious way to increase your metabolism, and the more you do the more energy you'll spend. You can start today and the effects are immediate. Before you say, 'I don't have the time to exercise', you need to know that just moving your body more can help. Being more active can mean sitting less and standing more, driving less and walking more for short trips (and always taking the stairs rather than the escalator), or taking time for active recreation such as gardening or visiting the park. If you do some high-intensity exercise, you will continue to spend energy for hours after you stop exercising.

Boosting your metabolism is within your reach and one example of when it's good to spend up big!

KEY INFO Your metabolic rate (metabolism) is how many kilojoules/calories you burn each day. This is influenced by your lean body mass: more muscle increases metabolism. Eating more and exercise also increases metabolism.

Long story short You can boost your metabolism by building muscle and exercising.

Hungry for more? Calculate your theoretical daily kilojoule needs at www.weightloss.com.au/weight-loss-tools or www.mayoclinic.com/health/calorie-calculator/NU00598. Some dietitians can hook you up to a machine that calculates your kilojoule daily needs more accurately.

⏵ Eating late at night makes you fat

It's difficult to live by the old adage 'breakfast like a king, lunch like a prince, and dine like a pauper'. The reality is that many of us enjoy our main meal in the evening when the travails of the day are behind us. Is this making us fat? Looking at the science overall, the answer is no. When it comes to weight, the overarching principle is the balance between the kilojoules /calories consumed versus the amount of energy used through physical activity. There are no studies to suggest that eating late at night causes weight gain. However, there are possible reasons why big dinners and late-night snacks may not be the best idea.

We know that our natural circadian rhythm prefers night for sleeping and not eating. Shift workers who turn their body clocks upside down tend to be heavier and at higher risk for cardiovascular disease—studies suggest that their insulin levels are higher in the evenings, and the effect of insulin in encouraging body fat storage is well known. Although this may be a plausible explanation for the idea that eating at night makes you fat, we just don't have the research to provide a conclusive answer just yet. But do we really need to do it? Many people find they sleep better and feel fresher the morning after a lighter evening meal—try it for yourself and see.

Practically speaking, eating less at night may help you eat less overall, and perhaps curb that late-night TV and chocolate/biscuit/ice cream habit. Choosing the right foods at night can also help control blood glucose levels. Low-GI foods (see page 46) at the evening meal can reduce the glycemic response (impact of blood glucose levels) to breakfast the next day, a phenomenon known as the 'second-meal effect'. Eating less at night may also create a new desire for breakfast. It's a good thing to wake up hungry. Stoke your metabolic furnace with a low-GI breakfast such as oat porridge, grainy toast or a fruit smoothie and you'll experience better blood glucose levels and less hunger through the morning.

When it comes to your dinner, don't get too tied up with timetables, but rather focus on eating lots of vegetables or salad, low-GI carbs, and modest portions of lean protein (for example, meat, fish or chicken). Ask yourself: do I really need dessert? Perhaps finish off with a piece of fruit or a cup of herb tea. And remember, humans are marvellously adaptable. Culture, tradition and lifestyle are powerful influencers on our eating habits—just ask the Spanish who frequently dine late at night and sleep in the afternoons!

KEY INFO The amount of food you eat is important for weight control, not the time you eat it. Snacking on high-kilojoule foods in the evening is not helpful in maintaining a healthy weight.

LONG STORY SHORT Eat regular meals through the day. Enjoy a balanced dinner but try not to pig out in front of the TV afterwards.

HUNGRY FOR MORE? Do some stretches in front of the TV rather than snack—here's how: www.mayoclinic.com/health/stretching/WL00030.

▶ Carbs are fattening

There is nothing especially fattening about carbohydrates, or 'carbs'. And, really, it is all academic anyway because we eat foods, not nutrients. Most foods contain a mixture of carbs, fats and proteins. However, let's continue down the academic path.

Any food can be fattening if you overeat. It doesn't seem to matter a whole lot whether your food is high in fat or carbs, but how much you eat in total (that is, kilojoules/calories). Pure carbs have the same number of kilojoules per gram as pure protein, about three-quarters the kilojoules of pure alcohol, and around half the kilojoules of pure fat.

The 'fattening' potential of foods is now being talked about in terms of energy density, or kilojoules per gram. Eating a lot of foods with a high energy density increases the chance of weight gain. While there are high-carb foods with a high energy density such as crackers and pretzels, there are plenty of low-energy-density examples too such as potatoes.

To prevent weight gain, a food's 'filling power' is also important so you can eat less without feeling hungry. High-protein foods and low-GI carbs tend to be good fillers, whereas fat is easily over-consumed because it tastes good, isn't bulky and slides down easily! Which isn't to say you should stop eating fat to lose weight either, but simply to show why carbs aren't especially fattening (see *Low-fat diet is best*, page 35).

Carb quality is also important to help keep weight down, and some carb foods seem to be more fattening than others. Studies of large numbers of people (called 'population studies') have shown that drinking a lot of soft drinks (sodas) and eating a lot of desserts are associated with weight gain, but eating wholegrain foods seems to keep weight off.

So you can see that the story of weight gain or loss is far more complex than just carb content.

What are carbs?

Carbohydrates (carbs) are one of the four nutrients in food that provide kilojoules, or energy, to fuel the body. Carbs give us energy to fuel our heart, lungs, kidneys, brain and muscles. They are particularly important to fuel the brain to help us think clearly and balance our mood, as well as to power muscles during exercise.

Carbs can be divided into two main groups: sugars and starches. In fact, starches are made up of lots of sugar (glucose) molecules stuck together, and so when digested, both starches and sugars produce sugar (glucose) in the body. Glucose produced by eating carbs travels around the body in the blood and can be measured by a blood glucose level. Foods high in carbs are starchy foods or foods containing sugars. Sugars can be added as an ingredient, or occur naturally (such as in fruit and milk).

You can't talk about carbs without mentioning the glycemic index (GI). The GI is a way of comparing different carbs by ranking their effect on blood sugar levels. High-GI carbs cause a rapid rise in blood sugars (and need a lot of insulin), whereas low-GI carbs have a more gradual and longer lasting effect. Moderate-GI carbs are somewhere in the middle. The obvious benefits of low-GI foods are for people with diabetes who struggle to keep their blood sugar and insulin levels down at a normal level; however, lower GI foods have been shown to reduce the risk of developing diabetes in the first place. A low-GI diet may also help with weight control because low-GI foods tend to be more satisfying. Being a bit more selective about carbs and favouring those with a low GI has now become part of healthy advice for everyone.

Classification of GI

GI 55 or less is LOW
GI 56–69 is MEDIUM
GI 70 or more is HIGH

Choosing lower GI carbs

HIGHER GI FOOD	LOWER GI ALTERNATIVE
mashed potato (high)	parsnip (low)
jasmine rice (high)	basmati rice (medium)
white bread (high)	multigrain bread (low)
jelly beans (high)	orange-flavoured soft drink (medium)
rice pasta—made with rice flour (high)	orange juice, unsweetened (low)
rice cracker (high)	dried apricots (low)
	regular spaghetti (low)
	boiled potato (medium)
	4-bean mix (low)
	rye crispbread (medium)

*GI figures from www.glycemicindex.com

KEY INFO Carbohydrates are the body's main fuel source for the brain and muscles. There is nothing especially fattening about carbs. Weight gain is caused by eating too many kilojoules/calories from all sources.

LONG STORY SHORT Choose quality carb-containing foods such as wholegrains and low GI options in a balanced diet, and reduce the number of kilojoules you eat to lose weight.

HUNGRY FOR MORE? See www.glycemicindex.com.

▶ You need a low-carb diet to lose weight

The low-carb trend is the result mainly of fad-diet books. There has been research in this area as well. Several studies have been published in reputable scientific journals showing the effectiveness of low-carb diets for weight loss, and this has challenged traditional weight-loss advice. What we don't know are the long-term effects of such diets.

There are certainly good reasons to think low-carb diets are not a healthy way of life because they restrict health-protecting plant foods such as grains, starchy vegetables and fruits. What has been proved is that weight loss can be achieved in a much healthier way using a less extreme moderate-carb approach. The good old low-fat diet with a little more lean protein and a little less carb (ensuring good carb choices) has been shown to work a treat for weight loss and for lowering cholesterol and blood sugars.

The largest diet study in the world—a multi-centre European study called Diogenes—published results in November 2010 which demonstrated that a higher protein, moderate carbohydrate (low-GI) diet worked best for maintaining weight loss (although the study was limited to only seven-and-a-half months).

The brain needs glucose for energy (produced from the digestion of carbohydrates) and low-carb diets are bad for learning, memory, thinking and overall mood. Research suggests that restricting carbohydrates reduces the amount of energy available to the brain, thereby adversely affecting our cognitive ability. A study by Tufts University in the USA clearly showed low-carb dieters didn't perform as well on cognitive tests (mental function tests that deal with thinking, learning and problem solving). The research also showed that cognitive impairment improved when carbohydrates were put back in meals.

Foods we know are good for weight loss contain carbs. The lower GI values of most wholegrain foods and legumes is an important factor in weight control because they provide a slow and sustained release of energy, thus creating a feeling of satisfaction.

A higher protein, moderate carbohydrate daily menu

Breakfast	Wholegrain muesli (unsweetened) or oat porridge with low-fat milk Berries
Morning snack	Vegetable sticks and hummus dip or tomato salsa Unsalted nuts
Lunch	Wholegrain bread or crispbread (sourdough) Lean chicken, beef, turkey, tuna, salmon, sardines or egg Plenty of mixed vegetables or salad Oil dressing or margarine spread
Afternoon snack	Natural (or no added sugar) yoghurt Fruit (eg, apple, orange, pear, kiwifruit)
Dinner	Stir-fried lean beef, pork, chicken or turkey with plenty of vegetables Wholegrain pasta or noodles A little oil for cooking
Drinks	Water, low-fat milk, diet drinks

Milk and milk products have also been shown to help with weight loss (perhaps due to their calcium, but it's not clear yet) and they have carbs as well. You give up much more than you get with low-carb diets, so there's really no need for them.

KEY INFO Low-carb diets do work to lose weight; however, they are not a healthy way to eat. You can lose just as much weight on a more balanced diet moderate in carbohydrates.

LONG STORY SHORT To lose weight, cut back on kilojoules/calories. Eat a variety of foods from the food groups, but be selective in choosing the best quality foods from each group: wholegrain and low-GI carbs are best for weight loss.

HUNGRY FOR MORE? See www.glycemicindex.com and www.diogenes-eu.org/WeightLossStudy

⊙ Spicy food speeds up your metabolism

Many people believe they have difficulty losing weight because they have a 'slow metabolism' (see *I can't lose weight because I have a slow metabolism*, page 41). So it's comforting to think that breaking out in a sweat over a bowl of chilli is boosting your metabolic rate, thanks to its capsaicin (the chemical compound that gives it the heat). Researchers have found that capsaicin can boost heat generation and thus your metabolic rate, which means you burn more energy. But it's all pretty short term. And the studies are few and small (and some of them used supplements, not real food!). If you eat chilli often and don't go back for seconds and say no thanks to the sour cream, the benefits may add up. But there's no serious evidence that eating chilli (or black pepper or other spicy foods) work as long-term metabolic boosters that will help you burn excess fat.

Look at real life. They eat a lot of chilli in Mexico and that country has a major problem with overweight and obesity—although maybe it would be a bigger problem without the chilli benefits.

The good news is that boosting your metabolism is within your reach, but there's no quick fix. It's the usual suspects: healthy eating (at regular intervals) and moving more, including some resistance exercise (yes, weights) to get yourself some muscle power.

KEY INFO Enjoy chilli if you like spicy food, but say no to seconds and get moving for long-term metabolic benefits.
LONG STORY SHORT Chilli and other spicy foods may briefly boost your metabolic rate, but for long-term benefits you've got to eat healthy, move more and build muscle.
HUNGRY FOR MORE Search 'cooking with chilli/chilli' for recipes and tips.

⊙ Diet pills and supplements help you lose weight

There's very little real evidence that the numerous weight loss pills and supplements on the pharmacy shelves and seemingly everywhere on the internet will do much more than lighten your wallet.

But the appeal of easy and speedy weight loss is as hard to resist as the 'thrilled with my new body' testimonials, 'amazing' before and after shots and 'works fast—lose 10 pounds or 5 kilos in 10 days' promises.

The weight loss pills and supplements currently on offer work in a variety of ways, depending on the active ingredient/s, from decreasing appetite, increasing satiety and boosting metabolism to blocking fat absorption. Some of them have rather unpleasant side effects.

Fat blockers for example, which reduce the amount of fat the body can absorb, can cause flatulence, oily evacuation and faecal incontinence (so are not to be taken lightly). As they also block absorption of essential fat-soluble vitamins, you need to take a multivitamin too (more money from your wallet to their bottom line).

Amid the clutter of 'miracle' pills and potions and herbal extracts, there are a few products that show promise as an aid to weight loss, but even these can't deliver long-term results without your help—that's right, eating less and moving more.

If you are struggling with your weight and think drug therapy might help, have a chat to your doctor. Be aware that your doctor won't even consider prescribing a diet pill for you until you have actively pursued lifestyle changes (eating less and moving more) for at least three months and that whatever is prescribed will be as an adjunct to a diet and exercise program tailored to your needs.

KEY INFO Beware of diet pills and potions and their powerfully persuasive advertising and marketing promising a new you. Don't believe 'testimonials' (not even from family and friends). If you're thinking about trying weight-loss pills, talk to your doctor before opening your wallet.

LONG STORY SHORT The really natural way to lose weight long term and rev up your metabolism is to eat better, eat less and move more. Some drugs may help, but even the pharmaceutical companies that make them admit they can't do it on their own.

HUNGRY FOR MORE See www.mayoclinic.com and search for 'obesity drugs'; www.mja.com.au and search for 'weight loss supplements, Egger'; and www.nhs.uk/Conditions/Obesity/Pages/Treatment.aspx.

⊙ Obesity is all in the genes

Think of all those times people say 'you are so like your mum' (or dad). There's actually plenty of good evidence to back up the idea that our body weight and shape are at least partly determined by our genes.

Studies have shown that a child who is born to overweight parents is much more likely to be overweight than one whose parents are not overweight. Most of this information comes from twins studies—it's not too much of a surprise to learn that identical twins tend to be similar in body weight even if they are raised apart. Twins adopted out as infants show the body-fat profile of their biological parents rather than of their adoptive parents.

However, although our genes influence our shape and size, they aren't the only influence. After all, our genes haven't changed much in the last half century as obesity rates have tripled, so something else is helping to pile on the pounds. Enter environment—a way of life that encourages many people to eat too much (especially nutrient-dense foods) and move too little. And lifestyle is something you can do something about, although it is important to set realistic goals.

So, if you are one of those genetically programmed to be larger and the effort to slim down substantially is unrealistic, be as healthy as you can. You are better off being fat and enjoying a healthy diet than being fat and eating badly. The same goes for physical activity—you are better off being large and fit, than a fat couch potato.

KEY INFO Obesity is not inevitable even if your genes give you a higher risk because you can curb excessive weight gain if you change the types of foods you eat and move a bit more.

LONG STORY SHORT Play your cards right. Everybody is different. Accept the hand you've been dealt, and that much of your body shape is predetermined. Be realistic about what you can achieve. Aim for a weight that's right for you, your health and wellbeing. **HUNGRY FOR MORE?** See *Obesity is a failure of personal responsibility*, page 27. Also www.ifnotdieting.com.au; www.haescommunity. org; and www.bellybusting.com.au (for men).

⊙ Worry makes you skinny

Wiry worry-worts really give the wrong impression about the role of stress and weight loss. It's more likely that stress makes you fat. So what's the connection? It seems there are both physiological and behavioural factors at play.

For starters, psychological stress elevates stress hormones, the main one being cortisol. Over time elevated cortisol levels actually create more body fat, and in the most risky places (around your middle). But hang on, aren't stress hormones meant to help you 'fight or flee'? Wouldn't you need the body's fuel sources such as fat and glucose for this? Although it's true that stress hormones help liberate stored food energy at the time of the stress, the body goes into storage overdrive if you don't actually use this energy for fighting or fleeing. And it goes where the body can reach it in a hurry for the next 'threat'—in the abdominal fat stores around the waist.

Apart from making you fat, these stress hormones also create other metabolic disturbances, such as high blood pressure, adverse blood lipids and endothelial dysfunction (stiff blood vessels), all of which contribute to cardiovascular disease risk. So what's the antidote? If your body is hormonally set for 'fight or flee', then 'fight' apathy and 'flee' the scene and get some exercise—the best way to prevent stress-related damage.

Then of course there's that behavioural issue of comfort eating. How many times have you reached for the chocolates, ice cream or cookie jar when a big hug, a few bouts with a punching bag or a change of scene would have done the trick? Stress is unpleasant and many of us have a habit of soothing unpleasantness with a quick fix of something yummy—and at times like these, broccoli just won't do. Since childhood we've been soothed from pain of all sorts with something sweet, rich or just plain fattening. Of course there's nothing wrong with a little eating to feel better, but when food is the number one fix in our emotional toolkit, weight can get out of control.

Beating comfort eating

Like many problems, the first step is acknowledging you're a comfort eater—a food-and-feelings diary can help spot triggers. When you know what sets you off, it is then a matter of finding alternative ways to soothe your troubles. Taking more time out for things you enjoy, talking to a trusted friend, going out for a walk, getting enough rest and generally not overwhelming yourself with too many tasks can help.

KEY INFO So the message is stress less if you can. Flee with glee and a good pair of running shoes, and reach for cuddles, not kilojoules/calories, when the going gets tough. Your heart will thank you.

LONG STORY SHORT Worry is more likely to make you fat. And even if it doesn't, the anxious 'type A' personality or 'stress junkie' is at greater risk of dying from a heart attack or stroke. So, on any front, worry is worrying!

HUNGRY FOR MORE? See www.mindtools.com/smpage.

⊙ Nuts are fattening

This is one of those 'too much of a good thing stories'. Nuts (along with seeds) are nutrition powerhouses packed with protein, vitamins, fibre, good fats, minerals. You name it, they've got it. They've also got lots of kilojoules thanks to a high (good) unsaturated fat content.

We need some nuts. To keep your heart healthy, it is a good idea to tuck into a handful or two (depending on your energy needs) of unsalted nuts a day or have some nut butter on your toast. Or add nuts to your cooking—they're delicious in stir-fries and pilafs or sprinkled over the top of salads or stews.

Portion caution is the issue with nuts. They are so more-ish many people find it hard to stop at that 'handful' or small packet. So you have to find a way to stick to the recommended serves because overdoing it on a regular basis might pile on those kilos.

What's a serve of nuts?

A serve of nuts is 1 small handful (30g/1oz)—aim to have one or two handfuls most days, along with two fruit and five vegetables.

- 30 pistachio kernels
- 20 almonds
- 20 hazelnuts
- 15 pecans
- 15 macadamia nuts
- 15 cashews
- 10 Brazil nuts

- 10 whole walnuts/20 halves
- 4 chestnuts
- 2 tablespoons pine nuts
- 2 tablespoons peanuts
- 2 tablespoons mixed nuts
- 1 tablespoon nut butter

KEY INFO Great food, eat small amounts most days—portion control is the key. Share the packet, don't eat it all yourself.

LONG STORY SHORT Choose unsalted nuts and enjoy them raw or

dry roasted. Nut butters such as peanuts and almond and cashew butters are deliciously versatile—look for brands with the lowest sugar and salt content. Chocolate hazelnut spread is more of a chocolate spread with some hazelnuts for flavour—not the same thing at all.

HUNGRY FOR MORE? Visit www.mayoclinic.com/health/nuts/ HB00085; or www.nutsforlife.com.au.

⊙ You can lose weight with exercise alone

Running for 30 minutes: approximately 1687 kilojoules (403 calories) expended. Scoffing a chocolate bar in two minutes: 1430 kilojoules (342 calories) consumed. Surely devouring that chocolate bar you 'earned' after your lengthy workout is OK, right? Er, no. Your hard work running has been sabotaged by the kilojoule-laden snack.

Hundreds—even thousands—of kilojoules can be eaten in a matter of minutes, but these can take hours to burn off. Making the appropriate food choices can cut thousands of kilojoules a day with less effort, especially if you don't have the time to spend hours at the gym. For some people, it may seem easier to exercise than to change lifelong eating habits, but in my experience most people just don't have the time or inclination for demanding exercise regimens. A Cochrane Review of 43 randomised controlled trials of exercise for weight loss concluded that exercise alone leads to only small weight losses, and combining diet with exercise was more effective.

Although exercise plays the trusty sidekick to the hero of nutrition in weight loss, its powers should not be underestimated. Physical activity confers a variety of benefits for everyone—whether trying to lose weight or not. Exercise can reduce body fat and waist circumference, improve cardiovascular fitness and metabolism and prevent chronic disease. The American College of Sports Medicine and the American Heart Association recommend a minimum of 30 minutes of moderate-intensity aerobic exercise (such as brisk walking) on five days each week **or** vigorous-intensity exercise (such as jogging) for a minimum of 20 minutes three days each week. Cancer prevention experts say you should be doing at least 60 minutes of moderate-intensity exercise a day to reduce your risk. The harder your work out and the more vigorous activity you do, the greater the health benefits you get.

KEY INFO Kilojoule/calorie restriction is more efficient than exercise for losing weight. High-kilojoule snacks can take a lot of exercise to burn off.

LONG STORY SHORT Diet plays the lead role in weight loss, while exercise is the supporting act. A combination of the two is the favoured approach for long term and lasting weight loss as well as overall wellbeing.

HUNGRY FOR MORE? See 'exercise counts calculator' at www.cancer.org; or 'exercise energy charts' at http://weightloss.com.au.

PART 2

Food pariahs

There are some foods that cop a lot of flak. Some of it is deserved but, sadly, small grains of truth are all too often embellished to construct passionately argued smear campaigns. It is not accurate, fair or useful to heap so much blame on individual foods, especially when much of the criticism stems from misinterpretation of scientific studies or stretching the truth by businesses that have a stake in the deception. In some cases anti-[insert food here] campaigners are conspiracy theorists with too much time on their hands; or authors with a book to plug; or well-meaning individuals at their wits' end looking for a solution to a medical problem that has no easy solution. At other times, the demonisation of individual foods comes from health experts, frustrated at the explosion of obesity and diet-related diseases, who want 'easy wins' in the fight against the food industry they see as the enemy. If you hear individual foods being described as 'poison' to be avoided at all costs, take it with a large grain of salt.

Sugar: pure white and deadly?

⊙ Sugar causes obesity

The pandemic of overweight and obesity in the USA, Britain, Australia, New Zealand—and around the world—is a dire problem with big impacts on the health budgets and quality of life of those affected and their families. On last measure, 62 per cent per cent of adults and 23 per cent of children are above the healthy weight range in Australia. Despite obesity having a myriad of causes and requiring multiple solutions, the temptation to point the finger of blame at individual foods and nutrients has been great. We all want to believe that there's a 'magic-bullet' quick fix.

The paradox of less sugar but more obesity

Like the increases seen in every country in the world, the prevalence of obesity in England has more than doubled since the late 1970s. The latest Health Survey for England (HSE) data show that in 2009, 61.3 per cent of adults (aged 16 or over), and 28.3 per cent of children (aged 2–10) in England were overweight or obese; of these, 23 per cent of adults and 14.4 per cent of children were obese. Yet the UK Food Standards Agency (FSA) found added sugar intake had fallen in the ten years prior to the National Diet and Nutrition Survey survey taken in 2009.

In the USA sugar intake between 1980 and 2003 increased by 23 per cent (much of it in the form of high fructose corn syrup, or HFCS). In Australia sugar intake fell by 16 per cent at the same time as obesity rates tripled.

So, in Britain and Australia at least, we can't dump all the blame for overweight and obesity in kids and adults on sugar. Recent research by Dr Alan Barclay and Professor Jennie Brand-Miller in Australia highlights the paradox of sugar consumption and obesity. The researchers found that Australians drank 64 million litres less sugar-sweetened beverages between 2002 and 2006 (preferring water and diet drinks). They also found that the percentage of children drinking these beverages (between 1995 and 2007) went down. They point out that there is no evidence from either clinical trials or epidemiological (population) studies (see pages 11–12) that there's an association between sugar consumption and weight gain. This is not saying it's OK to consume high-sugar, nutrient-poor foods—but you can't pin all the blame for weight gain on sugar.

Is there anything special about sugar?

A more fundamental question is: is it physiologically plausible that sugar could more readily turn to fat than other foods or nutrients? The answer is no. The body's super-efficient fuel handling system will turn any surplus nutrient—whether it is fat, carbohydrate or protein—into fat for storage. Sugar is nothing special in this regard.

Another aspect is that sugar is almost pure carbohydrate and population studies show that high carbohydrate diets are associated with lower body weights as measured by BMI (Body Mass Index). Of course, sugar does hang out with some pretty fattening foods like biscuits, pastries, cakes and chocolate.

What about GI?

When it comes to talking about the effect of food on your blood glucose or blood sugar levels, don't let the word 'sugar' confuse you. Table sugar (sucrose) has a moderate (not high) glycemic index (GI). This means that it is digested and absorbed more quickly than lentils or apples or ice cream that are low GI foods, but more slowly than wholemeal bread, rice and most potatoes that are high GI.

The GI of a food is closely related to how much of the hormone insulin is released as well. This is important because the sugar-haters say that the release of insulin is to blame for sugar being fattening. Sugar is not especially insulin-releasing, and this theory fails to recognise that protein foods such as cheese and meat release insulin as well.

What is sugar?

Sugar is a carbohydrate (a part of food). So is starch. They are nature's reserves in plant foods created by energy from the sun, carbon dioxide and water.

The simplest form of carbohydrate is a single-sugar molecule called a monosaccharide ('mono' meaning one, 'saccharide' meaning sweet). Glucose is a monosaccharide that occurs in food (as glucose itself and as the building block of starch) and is the most common source of fuel for the cells of the human body. Fructose and galactose are also monosaccharides. If two monosaccharides are joined together, the result is a disaccharide ('di' meaning two). Sucrose, or common table sugar, is a disaccharide, as is lactose, the sugar in milk, and maltose.

SUGARS FOUND IN FOOD

Monosaccharides (single-sugar molecules)
- glucose, fructose, galactose

Disaccharides (two single-sugar molecules)
- maltose = glucose + glucose;
- sucrose = glucose + fructose;
- lactose = glucose + galactose

As the number of monosaccharides in the chain increases, the carbohydrate becomes less sweet. Maltodextrins are oligosaccharides ('oligo' meaning a few). They taste only a little sweet and are commonly used as a food ingredient.

Starches are long chains of sugar molecules joined like the beads in a string of pearls. They are called polysaccharides ('poly' meaning many). Starches are not sweet-tasting at all.

The forest, not the trees please

Rather than blaming sugar for fatness we need to focus on eating less overall and on the nutritious foods we need to eat most for health. On a practical level, there is no need to ban a little sugar to help healthy foods go down.

To lose weight, reduce kilojoule intake by eating less of everything (except vegetables) and ensure the foods you eat are nutritious. A little bit of sugar used to make healthy foods taste good is OK, such as a drizzle of honey on natural low-fat yoghurt or wholegrain cereal with some sugar added (see *What is a moderate amount of sugar?* page 71). Variety and moderation are the nutritional rules to live by.

How can you tell if a food is high in sugar?

Of course the most obvious way is to taste it, but what if you're deciding what to buy and you can't 'try before you buy'? You need to read the list of ingredients and look for sugars and all their different aliases, remembering ingredients are listed in order of amount. If a sugar is near the top of the list, there's lots of sugar in the food.

Sugar by any other name is just as sweet

These are all the names of added sugars you might find in food. Generally, any word ending in —ose is a sugar.

- brown sugar
- corn sweetener
- corn syrup
- dextrose
- fructose
- fruit juice concentrates
- glucose
- golden syrup
- high-fructose corn syrup
- honey
- invert sugar/syrup
- lactose
- maltose
- malt syrup
- molasses
- treacle
- raw sugar
- sucrose
- sugar
- syrup

And look out for creative marketing terms like 'dehydrated sugar cane juice'—yes, I've seen this on a food label. And, by the way, 'organic sugar' has just as many kilojoules/calories as any other kind, and no extra nutrients.

What do the experts say?

The World Health Organisation (WHO) and Food & Agriculture Organisation (FAO) in their 2003 report *Diet, Nutrition and the Prevention of Chronic Disease* say we should aim to eat less than 10 per cent of our daily kilojoules (calories) as added sugars. The average daily energy intake for food labelling purposes used in Australia and New Zealand is 8700kJ (2080 calories)—10 per cent of this is 870kJ (about 200 calories), which is up to 50g (1¾oz) a day (10 teaspoons). If your energy needs are higher, you can have a little more, and vice-versa.

The American Heart Association warned in August 2009 that Americans need to cut back dramatically on sugar consumption, recommending that women eat no more than 6 teaspoons of added processed sugar a day, and men should keep it to just 9 teaspoons. You might be wondering if this recommendation is relevant to you since it came from the Heart Association. Yes, it is important because it's about preventing heart disease (our biggest killer) not just for those who already have it.

What if you have diabetes?

If you have diabetes, a moderate amount of sugar within nutritious foods is OK (see page 77 for the myth *People with diabetes shouldn't eat sugar*). Kaye Foster-Powell, diabetes dietitian and co-author of *The Low GI Diet*, says many scientific studies show that a moderate amount of sugar in diabetic diets (for example, 6–10 teaspoons) does not lead to poor blood glucose control or weight gain. Keep in mind, however, that this moderate amount includes all sources of refined sugar—white, brown, raw,

What is a moderate amount of sugar?

The *Dietary Guidelines for Americans* say 'Consume fewer foods with sodium (salt), saturated fats, trans fats, cholesterol, added sugars, and refined grains' and this advice is similar to guidelines around the world. The NHS Choices website recommends that 'As part of a healthy balanced diet, you should eat foods and drinks high in sugars in small amounts.' *The Dietary Guidelines for Australians* (DGA) say 'Consume only moderate amounts of sugars and foods containing added sugars. But what does this mean? One of the downsides of providing vague advice is that we all interpret it differently. If you want to enjoy the benefits of a healthy diet, how sweet can it be?

The first thing to know is these guidelines—and others like them around the world—are aimed at added sugars (such as table sugar [sucrose], corn syrup and honey), not the sugars found naturally in fruit and milk. And here's the first hurdle when trying to translate advice into action by reading nutrition labels: the 'sugars' on the Nutrition Information Panel (NIP) of food products lists **all** sugars rather than added sugars. This makes the Percent Daily Intake (%DI) or Guideline Daily Amounts (GDA) of 90g per day almost impossible for the average person to use. You just don't know how much of the 'sugars' are added and how much are natural or 'intrinsic' sugars.

treacle, syrup, soft drinks (sodas), desserts, cookies, breakfast cereals or a teaspoon of sugar added to a cup of tea or coffee. (Note: a metric level teaspoon of white granulated sugar weighs 4.2g and is often rounded to 5g ($^1/_6$oz) because we don't usually level our teaspoons in everyday life.) And remember the ideal diet for managing diabetes is also the ideal diet for preventing it.

Putting this all together, if you want to err on the side of caution with your sugar intake, then limit added sugars to 30g (1oz) a day (6 teaspoons). If you have higher than average energy requirements—like if you exercise a lot—and are in good health, you can eat up to 50g (1¾oz) a day (10 teaspoons). This table shows you what this amount might look like in food terms.

Added sugars in a selection of foods

FOOD AND AMOUNT	GRAMS/OUNCES (& TEASPOONS) OF SUGAR
orange-flavoured soft drink (soda), 375ml (1 can)	49g/1¾oz (10 tsp)
cola soft drink, 375ml (1 can)	39g/1⅓oz (8 tsp)
caramel-nougat choc bar, 1 bar (53g)	31g/1oz (6 tsp)
orange cordial, made up as directed 375ml (1½ cups)	26g/¾oz (5 tsp)
1 slice lemon meringue pie, 113g	26g/¾oz (5 tsp)
jelly babies, 10 pieces 50g	25g/¾oz (5 tsp)
1 chocolate glazed donut, 60g	18g/⅔oz (4 tsp)
sports drink, 375ml (1 can)	17g/½oz (3 tsp)
1 tub (200g) vanilla low-fat yoghurt	17g/½oz (3 tsp)
chocolate-flavoured rice cereal, 45g (1 cup)	16g/½oz (3 tsp)

chocolate-flavoured low-fat milk, 250ml/1 cup	14g/½oz (3 tsp)
2 chocolate cream biscuits, 40g	14g/½oz (3 tsp)
1 small slice fruit cake, 40g	10g/⅓oz(2 tsp)
chocolate topping 20g/1 tbs	10g/⅓oz (2 tsp)
2 oat biscuits, 50g	8.5g/¼–⅓oz (1½ tsp)
high bran content cereal, 50g (¾ cup)	7g/¼oz (1½ tsp)
sweetened canned apple, 125g/½ cup	5g/⅙oz (1 tsp)

Figures from www.calorieking.com.au and the USDA database

KEY INFO Sugar is almost pure carbohydrate. It is broken down to produce glucose—the body's primary fuel source. It's not your body's number one choice for storing as fat (fat is). Sugar has a moderate GI (not high), which means it releases glucose (and insulin) into the blood at a moderate rate.

LONG STORY SHORT There's nothing especially fattening about sugar. Overweight and obesity in most people is caused by eating too much and doing too little. It makes no sense to paint individual nutrients as the bad guys. A healthy diet can contain a moderate amount of sugar.

HUNGRY FOR MORE? See www.glycemicindex.com; www. mypyramid.gov; http://dailyintake.net/di_intake_levels.php; and www.whatsinsideguide.com.

▶ Honey is better than sugar

Honey certainly has a unique and delightful flavour, but it is no better for you than regular sugar (sucrose). In fact, nutritionally they are very similar.

What's the difference?

Essentially honey is just another form of sugar. Like table sugar, it's a disaccharide (remember, two single sugar molecules—glucose and fructose—joined together). The main difference is the source. Whereas table sugar comes from sugar cane or sugar beet, honey is a sweet food bees make using the nectar from flowers. When you eat a teaspoon of sugar or honey the glucose and fructose yielded during digestion is used by your body for energy. How much energy? They are equivalent in energy value: 1600kJ (382 calories) per 100g (3½oz) for white sugar compared with 1300kJ (315 calories) for honey (these figures are different because honey has a higher water content so it weighs more for the same volume—a teaspoon of honey weighs 7g/¼oz and a level metric teaspoon of sugar weighs 4g/less than ⅙oz).

Is there more good stuff in honey?

Does honey have more micronutrients (vitamins or trace elements)? Even in 5 tablespoons (100g/3½oz)—a lot of honey in anyone's language—there are tiny amounts of a very small number of nutrients. These amounts are miniscule in the small amounts we usually eat and are insignificant in the overall diet. Honey does contain some antioxidants (flavonoids), and the amount depends on the floral variety and colour: darker honeys contain more antioxidants. An assessment technique called Oxygen Radical Absorbance Capacity or ORAC can measure the antioxidants: the results for honey are dwarfed by other commonly eaten foods such as apples, tea, strawberries, grapes and bananas.

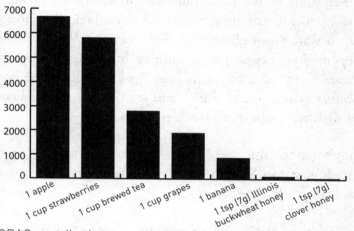

Antioxidant capacity of different foods using ORAC method

ORAC contribution per serve reported in μmol Trolox Equivalents

What about GI?

Most commercial honey varieties result in the the same or higher blood glucose level than table sugar (apart from the commercial product LoGICane). Recent evidence suggests that some forms of honey have a lower GI. These are the pure floral honeys that have been produced by limiting bees access only to some types of gum trees (eucalypts).It's possible that all pure floral honeys have only modest glycemic effects, but it is too early to say because there hasn't been sufficient testing around the world. A recent study reports that five German honeys have a low GI. The researchers found the glycemic index and insulinemic index (the amount of insulin released) correlated significantly with the fructose content of honey varieties. Romanian locust honey appears to have the lowest effect of all the honeys—but good luck finding this at your supermarket!

Why is this? Well, most commercial honeys are made from a mixture of honeys derived from different hives and different flower sources. To maintain a consistent flavour (so that the honey tastes the same every time you buy a jar of it), the manufacturer removes some of the more pungent characteristics. It may be the components that are removed are physiologically active and work to slow down absorption. For example, Australian floral honeys might contain alpha-glucosidase inhibitors that bees have extracted from the eucalypt flowers. We know that these potent inhibitors exist in many plants, and are the active ingredient in some diabetic medications (such as Acarbose).

Honey as medicine

Where honey does have the edge is as a 'medicine' rather than a food. Look at all these benefits:

- It's great for soothing a sore throat (especially mixed with lemon juice too).
- US research suggests honey may ease children's coughs more effectively than over-the-counter medicines.
- Because of its antiseptic and antibacterial properties, honey has been used for millenia for treating wounds and ailments.
- Manuka honey from New Zealand is a well known 'active' honey used in the treatment of stomach ulcers, gastroenteritis in children and fungal infections.

KEY INFO Sucrose and honey are both sugars and are nutritionally similar. They are both digested to yield simple sugars used for energy and have similar effects on blood glucose levels, although single floral honeys tend have a lower GI than sucrose. Any nutrients present in honey are in such miniscule quantities that they are insignificant, especially in the small amounts consumed. LONG STORY SHORT Use honey for flavour and enjoyment, not health reasons. It also useful as a sweetener in cooking as it dissolves more easily than sugar. HUNGRY FOR MORE? Visit www.honey.com.

⊙ People with diabetes shouldn't eat sugar

Do you believe that all chocolate and candy or lollies cause a rapid spike and then crash in blood glucose levels? You're not alone. If you ask anyone walking down the street what they think a diet for people with diabetes should include, chances are the first thing they'll say is 'no sugar'. It's one of the most pervasive and persistent myths about diet and health ever, I reckon. Yet it is a myth.

How it started

The collapse of the 'no sugar' dietary dogma began with the advent of the glycemic index (GI), which was developed in the early 1980s by Dr David Jenkins at the University of Toronto. The GI was the first measure we had to find out the effects of different foods on blood glucose levels. It turned the nutrition world upside down. Before the GI we separated carbs into starches and sugars, and recommended starchy foods over sugary foods in the mistaken belief they would not raise blood glucose levels to the same degree. We were wrong. Measuring the GI of a variety of starchy and sugar foods turned the old advice on its head. We discovered bread, potatoes and rice had a high GI, whereas table sugar and honey had a moderate GI. Even more shocking was that sweet-tasting foods such as (most) fruits, flavoured yoghurt and ice cream had a low GI! The shockwaves of this scientific development are still being felt. Even the terminology has changed. Using 'complex' and 'simple' carbohydrates to describe the speed of digestion is now defunct because we know many starches are very fast to digest and many sugars are slow.

The fall-out

The anti-sugar message has also soiled the reputation of all carbohydrates, and has promoted the low-carb diets. These diets cut out grains, fruit, dairy and starchy vegetables, a regime that poses obvious nutrition problems. The focus on avoiding sugar for people with diabetes encouraged a whole range of sugar-free products, many of which ignored more important things such as low sodium and saturated fat and high fibre content. A classic case of taking your eye off the ball.

All this doesn't give a green light to people with diabetes to stuff themselves with sweets, but it does discredit the 'sugar veto'. The advice for people with diabetes is now the same as that for the general population: consume moderate amounts of sugars and foods containing added sugars. The caveat is to spread your carbs evenly through the day, balance carb intake with medication, and choose low-GI carbs where possible. Sugar is **not** OK when eaten in large quantities and in less nutritious foods such as candy and soft drinks. But some sugar is OK when eaten in moderate amounts within healthy foods. For example, in low-fat fruit yoghurt, custard or ice cream, or wholegrain or high-fibre breakfast cereal—even a small piece of fruit cake or an oat biscuit. There is no need to especially restrict the natural sugars found in fruit and dairy foods. There's more to a diet for diabetes than the sugar content of foods, and a little sugar might help make healthy foods more enjoyable and life a little sweeter.

KEY INFO Sugar (sucrose) has a moderate GI and therefore does not result in sharp increases in blood glucose levels.
LONG STORY SHORT People with diabetes can enjoy sugar in moderation as part of a healthy diet.
HUNGRY FOR MORE? Consult www.diabetes.org.uk; www.diabetes. org; www.diabetes.ca, or www.australiandiabetescouncil.com/ Living-With-Diabetes/Healthy-Eating.aspx

⊙ Sugar causes hyperactivity

The scientific jury is in: sugar is not to blame for hyperactivity in children. There is no good evidence and no plausible biological mechanism for such an effect. However, food may still play a part in children's difficult behaviour—especially for a small minority of food-sensitive children. The issue may be where sugar is found—store-bought confectionery (candy), sweet drinks, cakes and cookies—because these products also contain food chemicals that may provoke a reaction in a small proportion of sensitive children.

About hyperactivity

Hyperactivity is now known as Attention Deficit Hyperactivity Disorder (ADHD) and covers a spectrum of difficult behaviours. It has a strong genetic basis and can be affected by a variety of physiological and environmental factors. A small number of children are sensitive to food colours and preservatives, which can result in adverse behavioural symptoms like those of ADHD. It is thought these chemicals behave more like a drug than a food on the nervous system of sensitive individuals, affecting mood, attention, concentration and impulsivity.

Which foods are to blame?

The idea that food colours and preservatives might influence children's behaviour was reinforced by the Southampton study published in the prestigious *Lancet* medical journal in 2007. It identified six colours associated with adverse behavioural effects in children: sunset yellow (E110), quinoline yellow (E104), carmoisine (E122), allura red (E129), tartrazine (E102) and ponceau 4R (E124). It could not conclude a specific effect of the preservative benzoate (E211). (The numbers in brackets are called e-numbers and are used to denote additives on food labels.) This study attracted worldwide media attention and calls to ban these colours in the UK, but it has since been criticised on methodological grounds, casting doubt over its conclusions. The amount of colours given to the children in the study was very much greater than children typically eat in the UK or abroad, and the effects were weak and inconsistent. The European Food Safety Authority found insufficient grounds to reverse the approved status of the additives used.

Studying children's behaviour is hard

Food and behaviour studies of children are notoriously hard to construct and control because children's behaviour is so easily influenced by their social setting, parenting, peer influences and individual factors. Perhaps sugar is found in children's party foods and they are simply responding to the expectation of being at a party? Maybe sugar is merely fuel for their childish energy? The myth about sugar and hyperactivity is so entrenched there is bias in parent's observations too. In one study parents were asked to rate their kids behaviour after a sweet drink that they were told contained lots of sugar—in fact an artificial sweetener was used instead—and they all said the kids' behaviour was worse.

Diagnosing food sensitivity is tricky

Another difficulty is food chemical sensitivities are difficult to diagnose—there are no valid blood tests (and don't believe anyone who tries to tell you otherwise). It takes the skills of a specialist dietitian and an able and committed parent (and cooperative child) to complete a program (called an elimination and re-challenge diet) needed to identify food chemical intolerance. Parents report their children's behaviour improves when they change to an additive-free diet and this is a good thing because they eat fresh and naturally nutritious foods and less junk, but it has nothing to do with sugar.

What else is there?

Emerging research is examining whether a lack of long-chain omega-3 fats are contributing to developmental brain disorders such as ADHD. Australian researcher Dr Natalie Simm has found up to 40 to 50 per cent of children with ADHD symptoms improved with omega-3 supplementation over a 30-week period. Part of the solution towards better behaved children may be eating more fish rather than hiding the sugar bowl—and it's good for their heart as well.

KEY INFO Some children may be intolerant to certain food additives that can cause ADHD symptoms, but there is no plausible mechanism by which sugar could cause such symptoms. Research into children's behaviour is fraught, highly subjective and difficult to measure accurately.

LONG STORY SHORT Food is not a big causal factor in hyperactivity, and sugar is not the culprit. Getting enough omega-3 may help improve children's behaviour.

HUNGRY FOR MORE? Are you food sensitive? Visit http://members. ozemail.com.au/~breakey/. For food intolerance see www. sswahs.nsw.gov.au/rpa/allergy.

⊙ Brown sugar is healthier than white

Brown and raw sugars are darker in colour because they contain molasses. Table sugar (sucrose) is derived from one of two main crops: sugar cane or sugar beet. Sugar comes from sugar cane grown in South America, Australia, Asia and Africa, whereas sugar beet is the source in the USA and Europe. Sugar beets look like large turnips. Here's how the different sorts of sugar are made:

- **Raw sugar** (99 per cent sucrose): crystals formed by evaporating boiled sugar cane or sugar beet juice.
- **White sugar**: raw sugar is dissolved and filtered to remove the molasses.
- **Brown sugar**: the brown colour comes from molasses, and is either produced by minimally processing of raw sugar, or adding molasses back to white sugar to make it brown. The darker the colour, the higher the molasses content.
- **Beet molasses:** iused for animal feed and distilling alcohol whereas cane molasses is used to make brown sugar and other darker varieties such as coffee sugar and treacle.
- **Golden syrup** is made by subjecting the sugar syrup to a process called 'inversion' whereby the bonds in the sucrose are broken so it becomes a glucose and fructose solution that stays liquid and does not crystallise—in this way it is similar to honey (although it has a very different taste).

The level of processing has little impact on the nutritional content of different sugars, which are almost 100 per cent carbohydrate. Some say molasses adds minerals to raw and brown sugar, but the levels are so small as to be practically insignificant—especially since sugar should only be consumed in moderation. You use darker coloured sugars like raw sugar and brown sugar for flavour and colour, not nutrients. The table shows just how miniscule the nutrient levels are, especially compared with the Recommended Daily Intake (RDI).

Nutrients present in 100g (3½oz) of different sugar types
(1 teaspoon = 4g sugar)

Nutrients per 100g (3½oz)	Raw sugar	Brown sugar	White sugar
kilojoules	1597 (381.7cals)	1552 (371cals)	1600 (382cals)
carbohydrate (g)	99.8	96.8	100
calcium (mg) RDA 1000mg	7	150	1
iron (mg) RDA 8–18mg	0.3	1.2	0
magnesium (mg) RDA 310–420mg	3	21	0
potassium (mg) RDA 4700mg	21	300	2
vitamin B-6 (mg) RDA 1.3mg	0.04	0.08	0

Note: RDA are Recommended Dietary Allowances from the US Dietary Reference Intakes (DRIs)

KEY INFO The only difference between dark-coloured sugar and white sugar is a little molasses.

LONG STORY SHORT Nutritionally, white and dark sugars are the same.

HUNGRY FOR MORE? See www.sucrose.com.

⊙ Only sugar causes tooth decay

Foods high in sugar can promote dental decay, but it would be wrong to lay the blame at sugar alone. In fact, any carbohydrate foods—including starchy ones—can be used by the bacteria on teeth to cause decay. Decay happens when the bacteria in plaque consume carbohydrates in the mouth and produce acid as a by-product. This acid weakens tooth enamel and 'holes' can form.

Digestion of starch starts in the mouth with the action of amylase enzymes in saliva, which break the bonds holding the starch together to release sugars. You can add biscuits (cookies), cereal bars, fruit bars, crackers, potato chips and pretzels to the list of foods that can cause tooth decay (also known as dental caries). Although fruit and vegetables naturally contain sugars such as fructose, they are not linked to decay.

Timing is everything

Studies show that how often you eat them is more important in caries development than how much sugars and starches you eat. Continual snacking prolongs the time teeth are exposed to an acid environment and it takes up to an hour for the acid to dissipate. Constant eating means the mouth doesn't have a chance to recover from the acid attack. Sweets (candies) are better eaten all in one go (and clean your teeth afterwards) rather than grazing on them over time. Slowly sucked sweets (including cough drops) are the worst. The best snacks for teeth are foods that actually protect against decay—these include milk, cheese, yoghurt, eggs, nuts and vegetables (crunchy vegetables are especially good because they massage the gums, generate saliva and exercise the jaw).

Texture is important

The stickiness of the food is most important. Foods that get stuck on or between teeth will cause the most trouble. For example, the sticky, stringy texture and natural sugars in dried fruit cause it to hang around teeth for longer, producing acid that causes decay. It's best for teeth to eat dried fruit with meals, rather than between meals. The 'cariogenicity' of foods and drinks (the extent to which they cause dental decay) contains a few surprises. For example, chocolate is not as cariogenic as other confectionery because its fat content and melt-in-the-mouth characteristic generates a lot of saliva which clears the sugars from the mouth and helps to stop the plaque acid attack (however, take care with chocolate containing dried fruit). Sweet drinks aren't as bad as sweet foods because they are swallowed quickly and don't hang around the teeth, although the acid in some drinks can cause problems.

The acid test
The new threat to teeth isn't about sugar, but the acidity of foods and drinks. Salad dressing, fruit juice, wine and citrus fruit are highly acidic and can wear away the enamel coating on teeth. For this reason juices are recommended to be consumed with meals and in limited amounts—especially by children. Products with re-sealable pop-up tops are a problem because they encourage sipping slowly over time and this pools the liquid around the front teeth for longer periods. A similar risk is posed by babies and toddlers sent to bed with a bottle—the milk pools around the teeth and can cause 'bottle caries', especially when they fall asleep and do not clear the mouth with saliva.

Soft drinks (soda) are acidic as well. Research in South Australian schools has found 68 per cent of teenagers have at least one tooth with signs of erosion, or acid wear, of the enamel—a much higher rate than teens in the USA and UK. Dentists say the problem is related to the high acid levels in soft drinks and energy drinks and their popularity with young people. Drinking them through a straw minimises their damaging effects because the contact with teeth is limited

KEY INFO The bacteria in plaque on teeth will feast on sugars and starches, not just sweets. Decay is caused by acid produced by bacteria.

LONG STORY SHORT Prevent tooth decay with good oral hygiene as well as limiting how often you eat sweet and starchy food and drink acidic beverages (and use a straw). Clean teeth after sugary or starchy foods.

HUNGRY FOR MORE? See American Dental Association website at www.ada.org.

▶ High fructose corn syrup is worse than sugar

In the nutrition world there is always a 'baddie' of the moment and right now it is high-fructose corn syrup or HFCS. A preliminary internet search shows a litany of dire health consequences if you dare eat it, from an increased risk of weight gain to diabetes and liver damage. Is there just cause to worry?

What is HFCS?

HFCS made from American corn is the most commonly used sugar in processed food and drinks in the USA (and the sole sweetener used in sodas/soft drinks). In some other places sucrose or cane sugar (from sugar cane) is used.

Sugar basics

Sucrose is a disaccharide, meaning it is composed of equal amounts of two monosaccharide (single sugars) bound together: glucose and fructose. HFCS is made by adding enzymes (similar to our digestive enzymes) to corn-starch to break the bonds between the glucose and fructose. Honey is similar to HFCS because it is also a combination of glucose and fructose monosaccharides. During digestion, HFCS, honey and sucrose produce glucose and fructose in equal amounts.

Fructose by any other name ...

The term HFCS is a misnomer because it doesn't actually contain high fructose levels. The name is used because pure corn syrup contains no fructose at all, but when treated with enzymes varying proportions of fructose are produced. The most common types of HFCS are 55 per cent and 42 per cent fructose (the remainder being glucose). Similarly, sucrose is 50 per cent fructose.

What about GI?

Glucose has the highest GI of all the sugars (99) and fructose has the lowest (19), and this is the reason sucrose (a blend of glucose and fructose) has a moderate GI (68). Although the GI of HFCS is not available, But there is no reason to expect it to be any different to sucrose. Lower GI foods are thought to be advantageous because they cause smaller swings in blood glucose and insulin levels.

Fructose

Interestingly, pure fructose has been available for years and used by people with diabetes to replace sucrose because of its lower GI and higher sweetness: you can use a smaller amount for the same sweetness as regular sugar (sucrose).

WHY IS IT USED?

Most HFCS in the American diet is consumed in sweet drinks but it is also added to dairy desserts, yoghurt, baked goods, canned fruit and breakfast cereal. HFCS is widely used because US agricultural policy favours corn farmers and makes imported sugar more expensive. Food manufacturers like it because it is economical, liquid and easy to mix, and adds good texture and sweetness to a wide range of foods. Many opponents of HFCS have issues with 'big agriculture' in the USA. I'm not a fan of high-intensity monoculture production either but that's a different argument. The question at hand is whether HCFS is more harmful to human health compared with sucrose.

IS IT HARMFUL?

HFCS, cane sugar, beet sugar and honey all yield the same 'simple' (monosaccharide) sugars during digestion. There is no reason to expect HFCS to have unique effects on health for this reason. Like all simple sugars, they are absorbed by the small intestine: glucose can be used for energy throughout the body, whereas fructose is transported to the liver for conversion to metabolic energy.

It is this extra step that attracts the most argument, because it favours the formation of body fat (called 'de-novo lipogenesis') during overeating. But this extra step is also needed for the metabolism of the fructose from sucrose as well. Since both sucrose and HFCS yield the same proportion of glucose and fructose, everything bad said about HFCS must also apply to sucrose—but sucrose is not demonised in the same way as HFCS. Body fat is only made when there is excess energy (kilojoules/calories).

Fructose can elevate levels of triglycerides (TG) in the blood and this increases the risk of coronary heart disease—depending on how much and how often the fructose is ingested. Large amounts of fructose are required to increase TG, and there is no effect at less than 133g (4½oz) per day—Australians consume around a teaspoon (4–5g) a day. The body also adapts to higher amounts of fructose and the triglyceride-increasing effect becomes less over time.

There are scientific studies showing detrimental effects of fructose—however, many of these involve giving pure (or very high) fructose feed to animals, a highly irrelevant scenario, and the effects cannot be separated from overfeeding with any sugar. Over-eating makes us fat and this is bad for our metabolic health but it is it far from proven that this is a specific effect of HFCS. A recent review published in the journal *Nutrition Metabolism* concludes 'moderate fructose consumption of less than or equal to 50g (1¾oz) per day or around 10 per cent of energy has no deleterious effect on lipid and glucose control and of less than or equal to 100g per day does not influence body weight. No fully relevant data account for a direct link between moderate dietary fructose intake and health risk markers.'

And what of the criticism that fructose reduces satiety and increases food intake? The scientific evidence on this is inconclusive, but indications are less than 100g (3½oz) per day has no effect.

ARE THERE ANY BENEFITS OF FRUCTOSE?

Fructose has been known for years informally as the 'diabetic sugar' and this is because it has a low GI. This is why most fruits have a low GI too—because their predominant sugar is fructose. Fructose has a gentler effect on blood glucose levels and evokes less insulin response—which is a good thing in terms of metabolic health and body weight. The other thing about fructose is it is 1.7 times sweeter than sucrose, so you can use less for the same sweetness.

WHAT DO EXPERTS SAY?

The American Medical Association calls for more research but says it is unlikely that HFCS contributes to obesity any more than sucrose. The *Huffington Post* quoted Michael Jacobson, executive director of the Center for Science in the Public Interest, saying sugar and high fructose corn syrup are nutritionally the same, and there's no evidence that the sweetener is any worse for the body than sugar. Even food evangelist Michael Pollan in his book *Food Rules* says 'high fructose corn syrup is no worse for you than sugar' but then says to avoid it anyway because foods made with it are highly processed.

A matter of degree?

The whole HFCS issue is clouded by the fact that Americans drink way too much soft drink, and this is a worry. Another possible concern is a study published in the journal *Obesity* that found US sodas (soft drinks) made with HFCS were higher in fructose than expected: on average 59 per cent and up to 65 per cent (much higher than 50 per cent in sucrose). Perhaps another reason to give these drinks a miss? Or perhaps they are using a higher fructose-content syrup because it is sweeter so they can use less.

The main issue is that HFCS is no longer being consumed in moderation in the USA. It is now being added in large quantities to many less nutritious foods and drinks, and these foods and drinks are being over-consumed. Nutrition academic 'big hitters' George Bray and Barry Popkin report in the *American Journal of Clinical Nutrition* that US consumption of HFCS increased by over 1000 per cent between 1970 and 1990. The problem seems less with the ingredient itself but how much it is being (over) used, and the agricultural policy that has supported its overproduction and flooding of the food supply. Too much of anything is not ideal.

KEY INFO HFCS is America's favourite sweetener used in food processing. The rest of the world uses mostly sucrose from sugar cane and sugar beet. HFCS and sucrose produce glucose and fructose in equal measure during digestion.

LONG STORY SHORT The American food supply has high levels of HFCS and soft drinks are the main source. Americans would benefit from drinking way less soft drink and other heavily sweetened foods. HFCS should be regarded as other added sugars—to be enjoyed in moderation within a healthy balanced diet.

HUNGRY FOR MORE? Visit www.sweetsurprise.com (HFCS industry site)

⊙ Artificial sweeteners are harmful

Artificial sweeteners (also known as alternative sweeteners) are the topic of many scaremongering emails and websites warning that consuming them will result in everything from multiple sclerosis to cancer. However, they are approved for use around the world because they have passed rigorous safety tests. Many are chemically similar to existing food components, and when digested they produce the same components as regular foods, or pass through the body unchanged. So the idea they are somehow harmful is unlikely. Humans are naturally drawn to sweet tastes by our primal survival instincts, but we could well do without so much sugar, considering many of us sit down for most of the day. Our teeth could also benefit from cutting back on sugary foods, among other things (see *Only sugar causes tooth decay*, page 85). Artificial sweeteners can help.

Although there are sweeteners that contain kilojoules/calories (caloric or nutritive sweeteners) in the form of sugar alcohols, I'd like to stick to what are called intense or non-nutritive sweeteners, such as aspartame, because they are the most talked about. They are called intense sweeteners because they are up to 600 times as sweet as regular table sugar (sucrose) so only tiny amounts are needed to give the sweet taste we like. This means we ingest only small amounts. They are found in 'diet' or 'no-sugar' soft drinks (soda), cordials, jellies, yoghurts, ice cream and desserts.

The European Food Safety Commission (EFSA) have assessed the large number of studies and approved the following sweeteners as safe to add to food (in Europe, additives have an E in front and are called 'E numbers'; the same additive numbers are common across the world):

- Acesulfame K (950): 130–200 times sweeter than sucrose
- Aspartame (951), two amino acids joined together: 200 times sweeter than sucrose

- Cyclamate (952): 30–40 times sweeter than sucrose
- Saccharine (954): 300–500 times sweeter than sucrose
- Sucralose (955) derived from sugar: 600 times as sweet as sucrose
- Alitame (956) made of amino acids: 2000 times sweeter than sucrose
- Thaumatin (957), a protein from the katemfe fruit (*Thaumatococcus daniellii*): 3000 times sweeter than sucrose
- Stevia (960) glycosides isolated from the stevia plant: 200-300 times sweeter than sucrose
- Neohespiridine DC (959) derived from a flavonoid in bitter oranges: 400–600 times sweeter than sucrose.

Food Standards Australia & New Zealand approves all those in the list above except Neohespiridine DC, plus:

- Neotame (961) 8000–13,000 times sweeter than sucrose.

The US Food and Drug Administration (FDA) approves:

- Acesulfame K
- Aspartame
- Cyclamate
- Neotame
- Saccharine
- Sucralose.

The reason for the international differences between approved sweeteners relates more to the speed of the (bureaucratic) approval process than to differences in scientific rigour. However, there can be differences in opinion in the interpretation of scientific evidence as well.

Aspartame, which has an entire website dedicated to hating it, was first approved in the USA in 1981 and is one of the most widely used artificial sweeteners. When metabolised by the body, aspartame is broken down into two common amino acids, aspartic acid and phenylalanine, and a third substance, methanol—all of which are produced after eating many common foods.

So do they cause cancer? There are animal studies suggesting some might; however, these studies involve giving lab animals **huge** doses that bear no resemblance to our intake of small amounts of sweeteners in foods. Food regulators set safe limits to use in foods and these have a wide safety margin. The World Cancer Research Fund (WCRF), the National Cancer Institute in the USA, and Cancer Council Australia say the evidence does not support any increase in cancer risk from consuming artificial sweeteners.

Some argue that artificial sweeteners do not help with weight control because they increase appetite, but this is not the case when they are consumed with other foods. A review found no good evidence to show how this could possibly happen. Sweeteners have the obvious advantage to people with diabetes of reducing their kilojoule and total carbohydrate intake. I think artificial sweeteners are a good choice in soft drinks (who needs the 10 teaspoons of sugar in a single can?) and gum (chewed after a meal, it reduces decay). I also think they save a few kilojoules or calories in low-flavoured fat yoghurt and dairy desserts.

KEY INFO Food regulators and health authorities around the world agree artificial sweeteners are safe. The studies that suggest possible harm are conducted on animals given huge doses and do not apply to human consumption.

LONG STORY SHORT Artificial sweeteners are not harmful. If you want to reduce your sugar intake, they can offer a sweet taste without the kilojoules. Used sensibly, they can also reduce kilojoule intake.

HUNGRY FOR MORE? See www.sweeteners.org (sweetener industry site) and search 'food ingredients and colors' at www.fda.gov.

Fat: friend or foe?

It's fair to say most health-conscious people are scared of fat and try to avoid it. However, failure to eat the right kinds of fat is a primary reason why our average cholesterol levels remain high. This is due in no small part to well-intentioned but misleading public health education aimed at reducing the risk of heart disease. Health authorities didn't think regular folk would understand the difference between saturated fat and unsaturated fat, so they went for the simple message to 'eat less fat'. As a consequence, the food industry went into overdrive in the quest to drive down fat levels, and shoppers sought out low-fat products. Rather than being a good thing for our growing waistlines, eating low-fat foods didn't make any difference and we continued to grow fatter. Some healthy fat is good, but the whole 'low-fat' movement has thrown the baby out with the bathwater. Although the emphasis in dietary guidelines around the world has now changed towards reducing saturated fat rather than total fat, the damage has been done. Here are just a few of my favourite fat myths based on 'errors of fat'.

Fat-free salad dressings are necessary

Home-made salad dressings are easy and simple: oil, plus vinegar and/or lemon juice, with perhaps some herbs, spices or perhaps mustard. It is fat-phobia gone mad when perfectly good oils are removed from commercial 'dressings' which are then loaded with salt, sugar and additives to put the flavour back in. Enjoying your salad or vegetables with oil is a healthy habit, and also enhances the absorption of antioxidants. The Mediterranean diet is certainly not low fat—and it's famous for its health benefits.

Reduced fat potato crisps are slimming

Potato crisps and the like were traditionally viewed as party food, to be enjoyed in small quantities on special occasions. Being so rich and tasty, and understanding that they were a high-kilojoule (calorie) treat, meant psychologically we knew when to put the eating brake on. Having such foods manufactured with a lower fat content has loosened our inhibitions and unleashed the impulse to eat twice as much. The other consequence is that because there is no fat to slow down the absorption of carbohydrates, they become high GI as well. The other bad news is that these foods are still kilojoule-dense (and nutrient poor)—and strangely unsatisfying: a recipe for over-eating. Switching to an unsaturated cooking oil to cook the crisps and reducing the salt is where the real health triumph lies, provided we can restrict our consumption of this 'sometimes' food to a modest amount (would removing the 'low fat' label help?).

You can eat chocolate, cakes and biscuits if you avoid oils and margarine spreads

Like the glittering hope offered by a subprime mortgage, saving kilojoules from healthy fats to spend on treats is a pipedream and will only end in a health meltdown. It's just bad dietary economy. And like subprime mortgages, kilojoules from treats are way too easy to get—restraint is needed. Considering how important omega-3 fats are for mental health, missing out will have you headed into a depression. While the occasional kilojoule sleight-of-hand is OK, if you usually skip healthy fats in order to indulge in nutrient-poor treats (often high in saturated fats), your diet is not healthy. Think of oils, spreads, nuts and seeds as another food group, like lean meat or vegetables, and therefore not inter-changeable with 'extra' foods or treats. There is no need to endure dry toast or soggy sandwiches—oil-based spreads (aka margarine spreads) are healthy, provided you select trans-free, reduced-salt versions.

⊙ 'Fry' food in water or stock to lose weight

There was a time, in the quest for eliminating fat of any type, when cuisine lovers the world over were thrown into misery by the advice to switch from oil to water or stock. Besides being a crime against cooking, flavour and gastronomy, and creating an infinitely inferior result, the advice was counter-productive for health. Cooking oils (any you care to name) contain good fats, fat-soluble vitamins, and healthful phytochemicals. Why would you avoid such a food?

KEY INFO Some fats are essential and healthy: the unsaturated kinds from oils, (trans-free) spreads, nuts, seeds and fish. You need to eat them for health and enjoyment.

LONG STORY SHORT Just aiming to avoid fat is not a healthy way to eat. Even if you want to lose weight, you can eat still eat some good fats.

HUNGRY FOR MORE? See *Low-fat diet is best for weight loss*, page 35.

The butter vs marg debate

When it comes to yellow spreads, there are three main types: margarine spreads, butter, and butter blends. Margarine spreads are made with a variety of plant oils, such as sunflower, canola, soybean and olive. Butter is pure dairy fat churned from cream, and butter blends are a blend of butter and some plant oil to make it softer to spread straight from the fridge. Hard margarines (known as cooking or stick margarines) are a different beast, solely used for cooking rather than spreading

▶ Butter is better than margarine because it's natural

I've done some consulting work for a company that makes margarine so I've got some inside information on this one. I've had long chats with food technologists whose job it is to tweak the recipe, and talked to topnotch scientists to sort through the evidence. I eat margarine myself, and recommend it over butter to my family and friends. With my conspiracy theory hat on, I'd say the wheels of the anti-margarine propaganda machine have been well greased by the butter industry! But I don't wear hats very often.

Margarine is made from vegetable oils, with just enough hard fat (often palm oil) to make it spreadable. It has vitamins A and D added (required by law), an emulsifier (often lecithin from soybeans) to stop it separating, a little salt for taste, natural colour and a preservative to keep it fresh. Sometimes a little milk is added, also for taste. Around 99 per cent of the ingredients in a typical margarine spread are from natural sources (the preservative is not). Margarine is not much more processed than butter.

To be fair, margarines developed a bad reputation because of the presence of trans-fats. These bad fats are produced when liquid oils are partially hydrogenated to make them solid at room temperature. However, when the science emerged that these were harmful, reputable manufacturers changed the way they made table margarine. Although many commercially used cooking fats are still partially hydrogenated, most table margarine spreads you buy at the supermarket are not. There may be a few cheap variants that still contain some trans-fat—check the label before buying. Avoid hard 'stick' or 'cooking' margarines because they have higher trans fat levels—use table spreads for cooking instead. The message about trans-fats is getting through loud and clear and the more we demand their removal, the more likely they will go.

Butter is made from cream and is almost 70 per cent saturated fats that increase cholesterol. Every tablespoon of butter is eating the equivalent of 2 tablespoons of pure cream—not milk—which is why it isn't part of the dairy food group. Eating butter and cream will increase your blood cholesterol and they don't give you any calcium. Butter is 80 per cent fat but contains no essential fats (omega 6 and omega 3). Although it does contain some vitamin A, so does margarine. It's a real 'sometimes food'—all about taste and nothing about health. The USDA calls it a solid fat and bundles it in with tallow and lard as 'empty calorie' foods to limit because of their adverse effects on cholesterol levels and heart health. Stick margarines are also in this group because of their trans-fat content.

Butter may taste better (as its fans claim), but it's a sometimes food to be used sparingly. Here's why. All its kilojoules come from fat and it will increase your blood cholesterol. If you like to do the numbers: 4 teaspoons (20g/⅔oz) of butter contains 16g (½oz) fat (including 10g/⅓oz saturated fat). In an average diet this would blow half of your saturated fat limit for the day. Add a 30g (1oz) slice of cheese and you've reached the daily limit.

Margarine spread, on the other hand, adds essential nutrients to the diet, including omega 3, omega 6, vitamin D and E. In the USDA MyPlate food selection guide, trans-free margarine spreads are regarded as oils that contribute essential nutrients so they are included in recommended eating patterns. Margarine spreads are an everyday food, albeit in small amounts.

For cooking, if you want a healthy result use a table margarine spread and for special occasions use butter. For everyday spreading, margarine is the healthier choice for the whole family.

KEY INFO Butter is high in saturated fats that raise cholesterol levels. Margarine spread is made from unsaturated vegetable oils that lower cholesterol and add essential nutrients to the diet.
LONG STORY SHORT Butter is a sometimes food for pure indulgence. Margarine spread is an everyday food.
HUNGRY FOR MORE? See www.csiro.au/resources/Margarine.html and www.choosemyplate.gov/foodgroups/oils.

⊙ Margarine is one molecule away from plastic

As far as urban myths go, this one is a humdinger! I thought it was very creative to even think of, but then I stumbled on the term 'plasticity' in a technical article about fats. Ah-ha! Mystery solved.

The word 'plastic' comes from the Greek plastikos, meaning capable to be shaped or moulded. In modern usage plastic refers to synthetic polymers which can be used in a myriad of applications, including bottles, sheets, fibres—anything you can think of. You might recognise names such as polyethylene, polypropylene and polyvinyl chloride. (PVC), or perhaps be more familiar with their recycling numbers 2, 4, 5 and 3 on packs. There is no similarity between synthetic polymer plastics and margarine made from vegetable oils.

Plasticity is the term in food chemistry given to solid fats that do not have a single melting point, but soften and turn to liquid over a range of temperatures. To a cook, the plasticity of a fat is its ability to hold its shape but be moulded with light pressure— which is quite important when making confectionery, cake icing and pastries. Butter has very little plasticity; margarine has more. Lightbulb moment: 'plastic' refers to margarine's physical melting properties, not to a similarity to the stuff refusing to break down in landfill and amassing in the world's oceans destroying sea life!

KEY INFO 'Plasticity' is a technical term describing the melting properties of a fat (which is different from plastic as a modern manufacturing material).

LONG STORY SHORT Margarine bears no similarity to plastic.

HUNGRY FOR MORE? Enter 'plasticity of fat' into your search engine for an education on the food chemistry of fats (but you will never get this time back and probably have better things to do!).

⊙ Canola oil is toxic

This is a good example of the adage 'you can't believe everything you read on the internet'. The overwhelming evidence supports the idea of canola as a healthy oil—it's high in monounsaturated fat (like olive oil) with significant amounts of omega-3 as a bonus.

Canola may not have olive oil's pedigree, but the rapeseed it comes from is a bright yellow flowering member of the mustard or cabbage family (the Brassicas). The 'rape' is from rāpa, Latin for turnip.

Canola oil was developed in Canada in the early 1970s through conventional plant breeding—that is, the girl part of the plants (stigma) were rubbed together with the boy parts (stamen), the same way home gardeners propagate plants in their garden sheds. It was not genetically manipulated.

As for the name: it was thought (apparently) that the word 'rape' might have negative connotations for shoppers, so the marketing gurus put their heads together and came up with CANOLA as in 'CANadian Oil, Low Acid'. The 'low acid' part is important in how this whole myth got started. The rape parent plant has high levels of erucic acid, which is toxic in large amounts, but canola doesn't—that was whole point of developing canola.

Although relatively new, there are many studies of canola oil involving thousands of participants: mostly they demonstrate the oil's cardiovascular benefits, thanks to its predominantly unsaturated fats, which include omega-3 alpha linolenic acid (ALA). The famous Lyon Heart Study carried out in France in the late 1990s showed an impressive 76 per cent reduction in risk of death or major coronary events (for example, heart attack, stroke etc) in people who had previously had a heart attack (and thus were at high risk) and who had followed a modified Mediterranean diet including canola oil-based margarine for 27 months.

Where did this myth come from? Call me cynical, but I think the mighty dollar is the root of it. The fats and oils market is highly competitive and there is always some who will profit from suspicion created about a competitor in the marketplace.

KEY INFO Canola is one of many healthy oils and spreads including sunflower and olive that we can choose from for health and enjoyment to help us to keep our cholesterol down. It's recommended by nutritionists and health experts, including the Heart Foundation.

LONG STORY SHORT For health and wellbeing (and to get the best results from your cooking), it's best to enjoy a combination of both polyunsaturated (eg, safflower, sunflower, soybean) and monounsaturated (eg, olive, canola, peanut) oils, depending on the dish.

HUNGRY FOR MORE? See www.canolacouncil.org and www.heartfoundation.org.au (/healthy eating).

Milk: essential food for humans or only for baby animals?

Milk seems to attract more than its fair share of myths. This is unfortunate as it puts people off eating enough dairy foods when they are an important part of a healthy diet. Most of us should aim for two to three serves a day as part of a healthy diet. In the case of allergy or intolerance, substitutes with added calcium are required. Considering milking a cow has such a wholesome rural image, it's strange that such a simple food can attract such a questionable reputation.

⏵ Humans don't need to drink milk

Dairy foods (milk, yoghurt, cheese) are rich in nutrients and have assumed such importance in our diet as to warrant their own food group. This is because they are nutrient-dense and provide a package of nutrients that are not found in the same amounts in other foods. This means that health experts and governments around the world have reviewed the evidence and concluded our health and wellbeing are enhanced by including dairy foods in our diets.

There is a lot to recommend dairy foods. They are high in calcium needed for healthy bones and provide the majority of calcium in the diet for most people. Dairy foods also contain a bunch of other essential nutrients, including protein, phosphorous, potassium, magnesium, zinc, riboflavin and vitamin B12. They have a low GI and help lower blood pressure when consumed in a diet with plenty of vegetables and fruits. Regular milk drinkers have a lower risk of heart disease and stroke, and emerging research is discovering beneficial 'bio-actives' in dairy such as lactoferrin, which enhances bone and immune health.

With so much to recommend them, why are there so many 'dairy-free' claims on food these days? Why do naturopaths seem to routinely suggest people avoid dairy foods? Why are there websites devoted to the 'dangers of dairy'?

Even though whole dairy foods do contain mostly saturated fat, this is easy to avoid by choosing low-fat versions, and limiting hard cheeses. Although some still believe milk is fattening, studies have demonstrated dairy foods may actually help with weight loss. The World Cancer Research Fund–American Institute of Cancer Research conclude that the evidence suggesting milk and dairy products increase prostate cancer risk is limited, and consuming milk probably reduces the risk of bowel cancer and may reduce the risk of bladder cancer.

Milk allergy affects up to 5 per cent of children at most

(and more likely 2 per cent), and 1 per cent of adults. Lactose intolerance is an issue for a lot more people worldwide; however, complete dairy avoidance is not usually necessary. The anti-dairy argument is hard to reconcile with the idea that humans have been eating dairy foods for thousands of years—the Masai tribes in Tanzania still live principally on milk, blood and meat.

What's the alternative?

If you cannot, or choose not, to eat dairy products there are alternatives such as soy milk and rice milk with added calcium. There are also soy yoghurts (check that these have added calcium), soy cheese as well as fun foods such as dairy-free frozen desserts. Life can go on when you're dairy-free, but it is a little more challenging to ensure your nutritional needs are met, and the taste can take some getting used to. For those who have chosen the dairy-free path, I'm sorry to say there are a plethora of websites also attacking the safety and goodness of soy milk (see page 154 on soy).

KEY INFO Milk is a nutrient-rich food and provides the majority of calcium in the diet.

LONG STORY SHORT Dairy foods are nutrient rich and low-fat versions are even better for heart health.

HUNGRY FOR MORE? Visit www.milkfacts.info.

⦿ Milk causes mucus

It's commonly believed that drinking milk causes mucus but when this has been studied in controlled conditions it has not stood up to scientific scrutiny. The thin coating you feel in your mouth after drinking milk is temporary and a result of its creamy texture. (By the same faulty logic, chocolate and shortbread are 'mucus-forming' yet no-one is blaming them.)

The other old chestnut is milk causes asthma, yet The Asthma Foundation says sufferers should not eliminate dairy without proper medical advice because less than 5 per cent of people with asthma are affected by food: the real triggers are allergens such as house pollen and dust-mite, respiratory infections and exercise. In a clinical trial by RK Woods and colleagues of 20 patients with asthma (10 believed dairy foods exacerbated their asthma and 10 did not) published in the *Journal of Allergy & Clinical Immunology*, patients were given a 'milk challenge' and both symptoms and lung function tests were recorded before and after challenge. The results showed that none of the patients reported an increase in cough or sputum production following the dairy challenge. Having said this, it is possible for milk to provoke reactions as a result of food intolerance rather than allergy.

Food intolerance (not lactose intolerance, see page 111) is poorly understood but is thought to occur when natural or added food chemicals irritate the nerve endings in different parts of the body, including the respiratory tract. These chemicals include amines, salicylates, preservatives and glutamates—none of which are high in plain milk, but can be present in some milk products. Symptoms can include asthma, sinus trouble and a runny nose.

There's a great diet book (with recipes) on the subject of food allergy and intolerance, *Friendly Food*, by immunologist Dr Rob Loblay, paediatrician Dr Valencia Souter and dietitian Dr Anne Swain. This team has more than 20 years experience and research in this area. They say:

There is a common belief that dairy products are bad for people with 'allergies'. In fact, this is not usually so. If you feel better avoiding dairy it may be because you've cut out the natural amines in tasty cheeses and chocolates or the flavourings in yoghurt, ice cream and milk shakes. Milk or wheat can sometimes irritate the stomach and bowels in people with food intolerance, but this will often settle down after the relevant food chemicals have been identified and eliminated for a few weeks.

If you think you have food intolerance, consult a dietitian with experience in this area for diagnosis. The condition is managed through the use of an elimination-diet-and-challenge protocol. There are no blood tests that identify food intolerance.

Avoid cutting dairy out of the diet until you have a proven reason for doing so because you might well be going short on calcium.

KEY INFO Controlled studies have been unable to prove milk causes mucus. Food intolerance may play a role in respiratory symptoms.

LONG STORY SHORT Milk is unlikely to be the cause of asthma or sinus trouble. Cutting out dairy can leave you short of essential nutrients found in milk

HUNGRY FOR MORE? See the book *Friendly Food* and www.news-medical.net/health/Asthma.

⊙ Most people can't digest milk

Lactose intolerance is when a person does not produce sufficient amounts of lactose-digesting enzyme (called lactase).

In the beginning

The fact that milk is a commonly eaten food throughout the world suggests we can and do digest it. The story of how this came to be is fascinating, and I was introduced to it by Glenn Cardwell, dietitian and fellow myth-buster, via Gregory Cochran and Henry Harpending's book, *The 10,000 Year Explosion: How Civilization Accelerated Human Evolution*. The authors reveal that the ability to digest milk in adulthood started around 10,000 years ago just after humans first started to keep animals for food. Geneticists believe by pure chance a mutation occurred that maintained lactase levels into adulthood and this mutation spread through the gene pool because it conveyed a survival advantage. That is, it provided an important source of nutrition that kept adults healthy and able to reproduce—and thus carry on the genes for digesting milk.

This ability spread though Europe and India. A similar scenario was also happening in Arabia where the milk came from camels. It was so successful that fossilised human remains shows 80 per cent of Europeans were able to digest milk 7000 years ago. Dairy farming is also highly productive per area of land and was a great means to support populations, ensuring its spread across the world.

How common is lactose intolerance?

A review by Gudmand-Hoyer published in the *American Journal of Clinical Nutrition* in 1994 reported the prevalence of lactose maldigestion was lowest in Scandinavia and north-west Europe (3–8%), but increases in southern and eastern directions, reaching 70 per cent in southern Turkey and Italy. Figures are also higher among people of Asian origin, Aboriginal people and African-Americans because of their divergence from the Indo-Europeans.

Is it all or nothing?
The amount of lactose that can be comfortably tolerated varies from person to person, but generally people with lactose intolerance can digest small amounts of lactose (such as the amount in a small glass of milk) without symptoms, especially if consumed as part of a meal. The amount of lactose in yoghurt is much lower because the bacterial cultures break the lactose down into lactic acid (giving yoghurt its characteristic tart flavour). Hard cheese contains negligible lactose. For the super-sensitive there are lactose-free milks and yoghurts available, and even lactase enzyme powder you can add to milk to do the digesting for you.

Intolerance vs allergy
There are those with milk allergy who must stay well away from anything dairy-based or they become ill; however, this unlucky group makes up less than 1 per cent of the adult population. Milk intolerance (which is different to lactose intolerance) also occurs but no data is available on the numbers of people affected, although it is expected to be higher than those with milk allergy (food intolerance is notoriously difficult to diagnose, requiring an elimination diet and food re-challenge supervised by an experienced dietitian—see page 109 on milk and mucus).

The risks of ditching dairy
Getting enough calcium is important for healthy bones and the prevention of osteoporosis as you get older. You might think there are negligble consequences to avoiding dairy foods but a study published in the *American Journal of Clinical Nutrition*

found people with lactose intolerance had a much lower intake of calcium because they ate less milk, cheese and yoghurt.

KEY INFO Lactose intolerance affects as few as 4 percent of the Caucasian population, but is more common in Asian, African, Aboriginal and Mediterranean people.

LONG STORY SHORT People with lactose intolerance don't have to stop eating dairy foods altogether. Small amounts of milk are OK, and yoghurt and cheese are well tolerated.

HUNGRY FOR MORE? See The Gut Foundation website at www. gut.nsw.edu.au; *The 10,000 Year Explosion: How Civilization Accelerated Human Evolution*, by Greagory Cochran and Henry Harpending.

⊙ It's easy to get calcium from foods other than milk

The reason dairy foods have their own food group is because they are good sources of nutrients that are difficult to obtain from other foods. The standard advice is to enjoy three serves of dairy food a day, where one serve is:

- 1 cup (250ml/8fl oz) of milk
- 1 tub (200g/7oz) of yogurt
- 2 thin slices (40g/1½oz) cheese

Each of these contains around 300mg of calcium. You can see from the table below where the 'three serves a day' rule of thumb came from: three serves of dairy a day provides 900mg of calcium. In fact, three serves of dairy a day is still a serve short for meeting the calcium needs of teenagers, women over 50 and men over 70.

Nutrient Reference Value (NRVs) for calcium at different ages

1050–1300mg (12–18 years)
840–1000mg (19–50 years)
1100–1300mg (women 50+ years, men 70+)

The lower figure is the Estimated Average Requirement (EAR), which meets the needs of half the population. The higher figure is the Recommended Dietary Intake (RDI), which meets the needs of nearly everyone (97–98% of the population).

It's difficult to get enough calcium in a diet without dairy foods. Not only are the amounts of calcium lower, but the calcium from plant foods is not as well absorbed. Grains, vegetables, legumes, seeds and nuts contain calcium absorption inhibitors such as phytates, oxalic acid and tannins. Non-dairy 'milks' with added calcium are good alternatives.

Non-dairy sources of calcium

Food	Serving size	Calcium (mg)
tofu (calcium set)	100g (3½oz)	336
soy milk (with calcium added)	1 cup	260
canned salmon (pink, with bones)	small (90g/3oz) can	260
prawns	¾ cup cooked (school prawns)	98
oysters	½ dozen (100g/3½oz)	90
spinach	½ cup cooked (100g/3½oz)	78
almonds	small handful (30g/1oz)	70
tahini (sesame seed paste)	1 tablespoon (20g/¾oz)	66
bok choy (Chinese green vegetable)	½ cup cooked (80g/2²/₃oz)	42
chick peas	½ cup cooked (85g/2¾oz)	38

orange	1 medium (130g/4½oz)	38
broccoli	1 cup florets (75g/2½oz, raw)	23
lentils	½ cup (85g/2¾oz)	10
Brussels sprouts	5 sprouts (100g/3½oz)	15

Figures sourced from AUSNUT nutrient database.

LONG STORY SHORT It's hard to obtain the amount of calcium you need without dairy foods. Non-dairy milk alternatives with added calcium can help.

⊙ A2 milk is healthier than regular milk

A2 milk is a new kind of milk available in the USA, Australia and New Zealand. The term 'A2' describes the predominant type of protein (beta-casein) found in this milk. Most milk contains predominantly A1 protein but A2 milk is produced by selectively bred cows. Holstein cows have a 50:50 mix of A1 and A2 whereas Guernsey cows have much higher proportion of A2, as do goats, sheep, zebu, yak and human breast milk. All cows used to produce A2 milk, and the A1 is actually a natural genetic mutation. Neither the A1 nor A2 gene is dominant so it is relatively easy to breed back cows with only A2—there's no genetic modification involved. If you are allergic to milk, you still need to avoid A2 milk.

The marketers of A2 milk say it 'may assist with your digestive wellbeing'. Proponents say regular milk's A1 protein may contribute to the risk of developing coronary heart disease, type 1 diabetes, autism and schizophrenia, and call it 'the devil in the milk' (and there's a book by this name), and they point to a particular protein fragment, BCM7 (beta-casomorphin-7), that result from the digestion of A1 protein. But the available evidence does not prove benefit from drinking A2 milk or indeed indicate harm caused by the ingestion of regular milk containing predominantly A1 beta-casein protein. Regulators who have reviewed the evidence agree.

In 2007 the European Food Safety Authority (EFSA) declined to do a safety assessment of A1 in milk, saying the evidence did not justify it. They concluded 'a cause and effect relationship is not established between the dietary intake of BCM7 (beta-casomorphin-7), related peptides or their possible protein precursors and non-communicable diseases'. Which is a complicated way of saying: relax because regular milk is OK. This is a real bummer for the A2 Corporation who developed and marketed this milk, but a win for scientific rigour and good old commonsense.

KEY INFO A2 milk contains mostly A2 type beta-casein (protein) and is produced by some breeds of dairy cow. Most milk has A1 protein. Proponents of A2 milk believe A1 protein is harmful and link it to diseases such as heart disease and diabetes—however, there is no evidence for this.

LONG STORY SHORT Marketers of A2 milk have invested a lot in the idea that their milk is better. So far, by scientific evaluation, it's not.

HUNGRY FOR MORE? See www.betacasein.net/default.htm (a scientific site from the A2 corporation), and www. foodstandards.gov.au and www.efsa.europa.eu

⊙ Raw (unpasteurised) milk is better for you

Smelly cheese lovers and makers in many parts of the world have been kicking up quite a stink (pardon the pun) because they are unable to buy and make local raw milk cheese.

This is because unpasteurised ('raw') milk is not permitted to be sold for human consumption because food safety regulations deem raw milk too high a risk to human health. Raw milk enthusiasts say we should be able to drink milk as nature intended, and pasteurisation kills many health-promoting components.

What is pasteurisation?

Milk is pasteurised by heating it to a temperature that destroys most disease-causing bacteria (63–72°C/145–161°F). It doesn't destroy all the bacteria and that's why you need to keep milk in the refrigerator to reduce their growth.

Why pasteurise?

Milk is a highly nutritious food for bacteria as well as humans and is known in food safety circles as a 'high-risk food' requiring special care to make it safe to consume. There have been reported cases of severe illness from consuming raw milk and raw milk cheese containing high levels of *Salmonella*, *Escherichia coli* and *Listeria*.

Milk and milk products provide a wealth of nutrition benefits. But raw milk can harbor dangerous microorganisms that can pose serious health risks to you and your family. According to the Centers for Disease Control and Prevention, more than 800 people in the United States have become sick from drinking raw milk or eating cheese made from raw milk since 1998. Heating milk makes little difference to the nutrient content, with the exception of vitamin C which is heat-sensitive—around one-fifth is lost during pasteurisation. But milk is not a good or significant source of vitamin C anyway so this is academic.

What's so good about raw milk?

Supporters claim raw milk is associated with lower risk of allergy, cardiovascular disease and improved growth and development of children. They also claim pasteurised milk contains decreased levels of vitamins A and D, B-vitamins and iodine, and the availability of folate and calcium is reduced. Reviews of the available scientific evidence by regulators have not supported these claims. Levels of vitamin C and thiamine are lower in pasteurised milk, but since milk is not a good source of these it does not pose a nutritional risk. We get vitamin C from fruits and vegetables and thiamine from breads and cereals, not from milk.

Raw milk supporters say it contains beneficial enzymes—probably to help calves stay healthy—and pasteurised milk destroys these. But it's hard to fathom why eating enzymes (which are proteins) could do you good when the acid environment of the stomach renders them inactive by digestion. Perhaps they exert their benefit between the mouth and the stomach? It seems unlikely. Unless you drink milk straight from the cow, the actions of these enzymes are questionable in raw milk too since milk needs to be kept cold to get it to the customer (enzymes are designed to function at body temperature).

Say cheese!

Enzymes and some harmless (perhaps even beneficial) bacteria do contribute to flavour complexity in raw milk cheeses. However, even cheesemakers admit you can make darn good cheese using pasteurised milk. Having said this, raw milk cheeses have been eaten for an age without causing illness. This is likely due to the composition and ageing process involved in making hard cheese. Ageing reduces the moisture content and pH, and this, combined with the high salt content, makes it hard for bacteria to survive.

Safety is in your hands

Whether your milk is pasteurised, or your cheese is made from raw milk or not, the way you handle dairy foods in the home is important in reducing the risk of food-borne illness (aka food poisoning). Keep dairy foods cold, pay attention to date marking and practise good kitchen hygiene by washing your hands and equipment with soapy water.

KEY INFO Milk is a high-risk food for the growth of illness-causing bacteria. Pasteurisation kills most of these. The process of making hard cheese from raw milk makes bacterial growth difficult because of low moisture content, lower pH and high salt content.

LONG STORY SHORT Drinking raw milk is a health risk. Any health benefits from consuming raw milk are not supported scientifically. Delicious cheese can be made from pasteurised milk, but safe hard cheese can arguably be made from raw milk. Care is needed in handling any dairy product to keep it safe to eat.

HUNGRY FOR MORE? See US Food & Drug Association fact sheet at www.fda.gov—search 'unpasteurised milk'.

⊙ Goat's milk is better than cow's milk

Goat's milk is consumed around the world and is the main milk in places that are not suitable for raising dairy cows. Their feed flexibility makes goats great for environments unsuitable for cows. Being smaller animals, they are easier to manage and require less land.

You may know someone who chooses to drink goat's milk, or buys it for their children in the belief it is easier to digest or better for people with milk allergy or intolerance. Goats' milk is just another kind of milk. It makes delicious cheese and has a unique slightly salty taste, but claims about its health benefits are overblown.

What's the difference?

The protein, fat and carbohydrate (sugar) content of cow's and goat's milk is practically the same.

Advocates say the fat globules are smaller in goat's milk and the fat does not separate, so it does not need homogenisation. They say this makes it easier to digest. However, cow's milk is homogenised (forced under pressure through a filter with very small holes) to spread the fat evenly through the milk and reduce the fat globule size—the fat globules end up being smaller than those in goat's milk. They say the proteins are different too, although some online information is incorrect. I have read that cow's milk does not have beta-casein and goat's milk does—this is incorrect: both milks contain beta-casein. I've also read that the main allergy-causing protein in cow's milk is alpha S1 protein and that it is not in goat's milk—but it is, although in smaller amounts; however, both milks contain the allergenic protein beta-lactoglobulin. Goat's milk is no less allergenic. In fact, there have been cases of allergy to goat's milk but not to cow's milk, and the alpha S1 and S2 proteins as well as beta-lactoglobulin were found to be triggers.

Nutrition composition of cow's vs goat's milk

Nutrients per 100g	Cow's milk (NUTTAB)	Goat's Milk (USDA)
energy (kj)	293	288
protein (g)	3.5	3.6
fat (g)	3.5	4.1
lactose (g)	6.5	4.5
calcium (mg)	107	134
phosphorous (mg)	92	111
selenium (ug)	1.4	1.4
riboflavin (B2, mg)	0.218	0.138
B12 (ug)	0.6	0.07
retinol (vitamin A, ug)	50	56
monounsaturated fats (g)	0.92	1.1
polyunsaturated fats (g)	0.1	0.15
saturated fats (g)	2.3	2.7
cholesterol (mg)	11	11
zinc	0.35	0.3

Source: NUTTAB 2010 and USDA.

Unlike cow's milk, unpasteurised goat milk is available but there are health risks associated with drinking raw milk of any kind and the health benefits are overstated (see *Raw milk is better for you*, page 119).

Most children allergic to cow's milk will also be allergic to goat's milk so it is not a suitable substitute. A consensus statement from paediatricians adopted by the Royal College of Paediatrics and Child Health says that goat's milk-based infant formula is not recommended for babies with cow's milk allergy and say soy, hydrolysed or amino acid-based formulas should be used instead. They also say goat's milk should not be given to children with cow's milk allergy.

Some parents are adamant their children tolerate goat's milk better than cow's milk. It may be a classic case of the placebo effect – what they believe comes true. In any case, provided it is pasteurised, drinking goat's milk poses no nutritional risk. I just wish goat's milk proponents would lay off criticising the cow's milk the rest of us choose to drink.

KEY INFO Cow's milk and goat's milk are nutritionally similar. They both contain proteins that can cause milk allergy.

LONG STORY SHORT Goat's milk offers no nutritional benefits over cow's milk—it's a personal choice.

HUNGRY FOR MORE? See American Academy of Allergy Asthma and Immunology at www.aaaai.org; www.worldallergy.org and click on 'Global allergy web links; and www.allergy.org.au and search for 'milk allergy'.

Meat: essential food or harmful indulgence?

While we can survive without it, meat is a highly nutritious food that provides essential nutrients, such as iron, zinc and vitamin B12, which are more difficult to obtain from plant foods. Eating meat was the reason modern humans evolved to have such a large brain and occupy the top of the Earth's food chain. It is unrealistic to think we will stop eating meat to save the environment; however, we can produce meat in a more sustainable and ethical way, and eat less to minimise our environmental impact. Meat-haters are quick to offload the troubles of the world onto meat—and it's true that livestock do contribute to environmental problems—but anti-meat arguments are simplistic and ideological. We need pragmatic solutions for a world that is hungry for protein.

⊙ Meat is bad for the planet

The global threat of climate change is the most diabolical of our time. The challenge of reducing carbon pollution is significant and complex. As well as the burning of fossil fuels and deforestation, the finger of blame has been pointed at the methane produced from ruminant animals such as cattle and sheep. Although ruminants do produce methane, which is a greenhouse gas (GHG), the environmental argument against meat has been infused with emotion and ideology as to whether human beings should eat meat at all.

There is little doubt about the rampantly excessive consumption of meat in rich countries and the environmentally damaging effects of factory farming. It is interesting that the carbon pollution from burning fossil fuels dwarfs that of pollution from ruminant animals, but the fossil fuel industry has deeper pockets than farmers. Like many food and environmental issues, it is not simple or easy to solve. The environmental impact of producing meat depends on where and how it is produced, and how much we eat. Rather than saying meat has to go, we need to think about how we can produce it sustainably, and put it in its rightful place as a sideshow rather than the main event on our dinner plates. Like many dilemmas within climate change, we have to weigh up the benefits as well as the costs—going back to being hunter-gatherers is not an option.

Greenhouse gases

Each year, agriculture emits 10 to 12 per cent of the total estimated GHG emissions. Discussions about GHG emissions from agriculture focus on the carbon pollution going out but often fail to acknowledge that carbon is also captured and stored by plants and soil on farms. This is called carbon sequestration. Australia's red meat industry is leading the way in having one of the lowest carbon emissions in the world and it has done

Land use

Cattle, sheep and goats can be produced on land that is unsuitable for growing crops. They convert inedible grass into nutritious food. Good agricultural management puts land to best use. This is also best for farm profits, and the farmer.

However, if there is large demand for meat then the agricultural economy will change to meet it. This is how every one of us plays a part. America's desire for burgers and (huge) steaks has created the phenomenon of feed-lot production and fattening cattle for slaughter on grain that could otherwise be eaten by people. And the land used to grow cattle feed could have been used to grow nutritious crops. The huge volumes of waste-generated feedlots means the natural nutrient cycling that occurs in pasture grazing systems is not possible, and instead the effluent produces even more greenhouse gases

Clearing land for grazing has been a major cause of deforestation throughout the world and this must stop: forests help to absorb carbon dioxide and reduce climate change, and provide habitat for the majority of animals and plant species on Earth. We also need to incorporate growing trees into grazing systems to capture carbon and preserve soil and ecosystems. The boffins say we need more integrated plant and animal farming systems that require fewer inputs—organic farms are a good example of this principle.

---

this by looking at improved feed digestibility, selective breeding and enhanced sequestration. Interestingly, speeding up the time it takes to reach slaughter weight reduces GHG emissions: grain-feeding at the end of life as well as the use of growth-promotants (hormones) can help achieve this. Although grass-fed beef requires fewer inputs, it is not an open and shut case that it is environmentally superior (see *Hormones in beef are harmful*, page 138).

Some perspective

High protein weight loss diets (such as the Atkins diet) have been criticised for recommending large amounts of meat and this is well deserved. However, more balanced and moderate higher protein diets are not as bad for the environment as you might think. Their saving grace is that they contain less food (kilojoules/calories) overall, and they limit energy-dense, nutrient-poor foods with a high environmental footprint. The weight loss achieved on such diets is a benefit to the environment because slimmer people eat less food overall and thus have a lower environmental footprint.

Water

You've probably heard the oft-used statistic that is takes 50,000 litres (11,000 gallons) of water to produce a kilogram (2lb) of beef. This sounds impossibly high—and it is. This is a classic case of manipulating the numbers to make things look worse than they are and a misuse of water accounting methods. Australian research has found it takes from 27 to 540 litres to produce a kilogram of beef in Australian production systems.

There's less talk about the environmental impact of sheep because they require less water, can graze on less fertile land, and are more efficient at converting feed to meat.

Nutrition

Meat from any source is nutrient-rich. However, red meat— which attracts the most enviro-bashing—is an excellent source of essential nutrients that are difficult to obtain elsewhere. Specifically, red meat is rich in iron necessary for healthy blood, zinc required for immunity and vitamin B12 for healthy DNA and cell division.

How much meat do we eat?

COUNTRY	AMOUNT OF MEAT RECOMMENDED FOR HEALTH (ADULTS) PER DAY	AMOUNT OF MEAT CONSUMED PER PERSON (ADULTS) PER DAY
United Kingdom red meat	70g	*average:* 76g/2½oz *men:* 96g/3½oz *women:* 59g/2oz
Australia red meat	65g/2⅓oz	77g /2¾oz
Australia other meats and meat alternatives	100g/3½oz	70g/2½oz
Australia total meat and alternatives	165g/5¾oz	147g/5¼oz
USA total meat	*men:* 170g/6oz *women:* 140g/5oz	*adult average:* 196.9g/7oz (all meats and fish) 108g/4oz (red meat)

NOTES: The USDA does not specify how much meat should be red meat in their recommendations. UK data from National Diet and Nutrition Survey (NDNS 2003), USDA data is national availability of meat, boneless weights (2008). Australian figures are consumption data from National Nutrition Survey (1995).

Sure, there are vegetarians who thrive on a meatless diet, but there are also those who don't and have to take nutrient supplements to make up the shortfall. The degree of difficulty for a meatless diet is much higher than for an omnivorous diet. In poor countries where people cannot afford to eat meat, iron-deficiency anaemia is one of the most common childhood diseases. Large nations undergoing economic development are also demanding more meat, so it is more urgent than ever to build sustainability into meat productions systems around the world.

The table on page 129 shows American men are eating more meat than they need for good health—the USDA says 20 per cent more; but women in the USA are eating less than they should. According to the NHMRC (Australia), the picture is more mixed. We need to eat a little more meat, but less of it as red meat—especially men. Although red meat has a masculine image, it is women who need to eat it regularly to meet their high iron needs. You might be surprised that Australians need to eat more meat, but they need to eat more nutritious core foods in general, and less nutrient-poor 'extras' or 'junk' food.

Game meats

Game meats, such as deer (venison), kangaroo, boar, buffalo and rabbit are highly nutritious and much more environmentally friendly because they are wild and require no agricultural inputs. However, they are not produced at a level that offers a realistic solution to world food needs. There are growing industries farming game animals, but they are still niche markets and require the same attention to sustainability as cattle farms.

Key info Ruminant animals such as cattle and sheep produce methane, a potent greenhouse gas. Plants and soil can capture and store carbon on farms and these can mitigate carbon emissions. People in rich countries eat more meat than they need.

LONG STORY SHORT Meat is nutritionally important, but some of us should eat less. Eat less meat, and this will send a message to producers that they can use less intensive and more sustainable methods to produce beef. We need to focus on farming animals (and crops) more sustainably with minimal environmental impact.

HUNGRY FOR MORE? See *The CSIRO Home Energy Saving Handbook: How to save energy, save money and reduce your carbon footprint*; www.redmeatgreenfacts.com.au (meat industry site); also Livestock's Long Shadow at www.fao.org and www.mypyramid.gov/pyramid/meat_counts.html.

ⓅMeat causes cancer

In some studies, eating meat has been flagged as a potential contributor to some cancers, but the scientific story is far from ending and is very complex. It may be too much meat, processed meat, charred meat or not enough protective plant foods, rather than meat per se that poses a risk. To say 'meat causes cancer' is an overstatement and scaremongering about a highly nutritious food.

Is there just cause?

Just because two things happen together does not prove a cause and effect relationship. An association—for example, people who eat lots of meat experience higher rates of bowel cancer—does not mean meat is the cause. The association may be due to other factors: for example, meat eaters don't eat as many vegetables, or meat eaters don't exercise as much. Good research methods take these other factors into account as much as possible but cannot completely account for factors they don't yet know about.

The word 'cause' has a very strict definition in medical and health research. For causality to be proven, the association must be strong, consistent and specific. A dose-response relationship must be present (in the case of a harmful food or nutrient, the more you eat, the higher the risk), as well as a plausible biological mechanism. The relationship must be tested and reversible (if you take the harmful food or nutrient away, the risk goes away). In addition, all other explanations for the effect must be considered. It's a pretty tall order, and eating meat has not met the requirements for 'causing' cancer. Some people say it is impossibly difficult to prove any food and health relationships and we should lower the goalposts to acknowledge that nutrition research is different to medical research into drugs. For example, it is ethically impossible and prohibitively expensive to set up an experiment to test the meat and cancer theory—it would involve studying a large group of people over a long time eating different amounts of meat and eating everything else exactly the same! It's quite different to testing a new drug for controlling blood pressure, for example.

What is the evidence?

The World Cancer Research Fund (WCRF) and the American Institute for Cancer Research (AICR) recommend we limit intake of red meat and avoid processed meat because they have assessed the evidence as 'convincing' that red meat and processed meat increase the risk of bowel (colorectal) cancer. However, cancer researchers the world over concede the scientific evidence is hard to disentangle.

RED MEAT	PROCESSED MEAT
beef, lamb, pork and goat from domesticated animals	meat preserved by smoking, curing, salting or the addition of chemical preservatives. This includes 'smallgoods' such as ham, bacon, salami and all 'sandwich meats', whether they are purchased pre-packaged or by-weight from the deli counter.

What is muddying the water?

Meat is a complex food containing a variety of nutrients. The nutritional composition can vary widely, depending on how it is grown, which cuts are eaten and how they are cooked. Fatty cuts of meat contain higher levels of saturated fat, so perhaps the cancer culprit is actually the fat rather than the lean meat—we're advised to eat our meat lean anyway for reducing cholesterol and heart disease risk. The problem may be charring the meat—carcinogenic compounds such as heterocyclic amines (HCAs) and polycyclic aromatic hydrocarbons (PAHs) are formed when meat is charred.

Population studies of meat-eating have used vegetarian groups for comparison, including religious communities such as Seventh Day Adventists (SDA). It is very difficult to separate other factors in these communities when comparing them with meat-eaters from more diverse backgrounds. For example, SDAs do not drink alcohol and their religious beliefs compel them to live a healthier lifestyle in general—not just to be vegetarian. Their religious faith may itself be a confounding factor for health. And then there is the big question of whether meat-eaters have less room on their plate for plant foods, which are considered protective. It may be a case of not enough vegetables, fruits, grains and nuts rather than eating meat.

How much meat?

The WCRD & AICR don't advise us to stop eating meat. Instead, they suggest limiting the amount of red meat to less than 500g (17½oz) cooked weight a week (70g/2½oz a day), and ensure very little —if any—of it is processed meat. This is 30 per cent less red meat than Americans eat, and only a smidgen over what Australians currently eat (77g/2¾oz a day at last count),   but bang-on the amount that government guidelines recommend for good health. The only arguments against this amount come from the meat industry, and especially from the smallgoods industry. The fact that well-loved foods such as bacon, ham and salami would pose a health risk has also been difficult for the public to swallow as well.

KEY INFO Interpreting research about meat and cancer is difficult—there are still unanswered questions. Prudent advice from experts is their best assessment of the evidence. Affluent countries eat more meat than recommended. Cancer prevention recommendations for meat are the same as government health recommendations anyway.

LONG STORY SHORT Meat does not cause cancer, but eating too much red meat or processed meat may increase your risk for bowel cancer. For this reason, as well as for general health, eat no more than 500g red meat a week, don't char it, and enjoy a diet containing plenty of plant foods. Oh, and you might want to restrict how much and how often you eat smallgoods, such as bacon, ham and salami (sorry!).

HUNGRY FOR MORE? WCRF & AICR www.dietandcancerreport. org.

⊙ Meat is fattening

Some girls stop eating meat in their teens in a desire to confirm to a slim body shape, and I suspect some older women do the same. They might talk about animal rights as their motivation but deep down they're also concerned about their weight. However, a meat-free diet may actually be counter-productive to achieving and maintaining a healthy weight.

How body fat is born

Body fat is made when we are overfed and the body cleverly puts some energy away for later, just in case we encounter a food shortage (as if!). However, it is unlikely that protein from food—such as meat—is converted to body fat. The body converts fat and carbohydrate from food into fat far more easily, thus the importance of ensuring your meat is lean—no white stuff on red meat, and no skin on poultry.

The power of protein

Protein actually takes more energy to digest, so you can probably knock off a few kilojoules from the total number on the pack, or listed on calorie-counting websites. This has obvious benefits for weight management, and also goes against the idea that meat—a high protein food—is especially fattening.

Of all the nutrients, protein is the most satiating (satisfying). It fills us up so we don't physically desire more food. Even in controlled scientific studies comparing different diets, people eating more protein report they feel more satisfied and find their kilojoule-controlled diet easier to stick to. Even the much criticised Atkins diet is effective because it is high in protein, even though it is not a healthy diet overall (it's not a balanced diet).

The power of nutrient density

In any weight loss diet, it is important to fit more nutrition into less food so that that fat —and not health—is the only thing you lose. This notion of fitting the most nutrition into the fewest number of kilojoules has resulted in the term 'nutrient density'. There have been a number of methods for developing nutrient-density 'scores' over the years, but in essence the more nutrients a food has in a fixed amount of kilojoules, the higher it scores. Meat—especially red meat—is a high scoring food.

Evidence into practice

The effectiveness of a higher protein diet containing meat was shown in the results from one of the world's largest ever diet trials, the DIOGENES study. This multi-centre European study found a higher protein, lower GI diet was the most effective for keeping weight off. Many other published studies have demonstrated higher protein diets are effective for weight loss and most of them have included meat as the protein-delivery food.

KEY INFO Meat is a nutrient-dense and satisfying food, but enjoy it lean (without the fat).

LONG STORY SHORT Meat is not especially fattening; in fact, it may be beneficial for weight control. Higher protein diets including meat are effective for weight loss in kilojoule-controlled diets.

HUNGRY FOR MORE? See www.csiro.au/science/Twd.html

⊙ Hormones in beef are harmful

A major food retailer guarantees its beef is free of added hormones. It did this because the general public finds the idea of eating beef that has been given hormones scary. But is there good reason for this? Beef growth promotants have been used for years in 20 countries and we've been eating the results in blissful ignorance.

Why are hormones used?

The word 'hormone' conjures up images of the oral contraceptive pill, boys growing breasts, shrinking gonads and infertility. But giving a male trans-gender person female hormones in order to feminise their body is a world away from the reality of hormones used in cattle. Hormonal Growth Promotants (HGPs) have been used for decades in the beef cattle industry in order to increase muscle gain, reduce fat content, and shorten the time it takes to reach slaughter weight. In this way they are more akin to steroids used by body builders and athletes to 'bulk up'.

Are they harmful?

This question is still the subject of a major international argument, with the USA, Canada and Australia saying HGPs are safe and the European Union (EU) saying there are safety concerns—they have banned their importation (mostly as a result of consumer lobbying). The World Trade Organisation (WTO) said the EU's arguments did not stand up to scrutiny because the majority of scientists around the world agreed hormones were safe when used according to best veterinary practice. However, the ban continues.

The European Commission say there is no clear link between HGPs in cattle and human health, and the US Department of Agriculture says the levels are not high enough to be unsafe for humans to eat. Food Standards Australia and New Zealand (FSANZ) says HGPs have been used safely in Australia for more than 30 years, and currently are used on about 40 per cent of

Australian cattle and annually add $210 million to the value of the beef industry. According to research by the European Federation of Animal Health, a person would need to eat more than 77kg (almost 170lb) of beef from an HGP-treated beast in one sitting to get the same level of oestrogen hormone naturally found in one egg (and we seem to have eaten those for centuries without harm).

What about the environment?

Although the use of HGPs might be seen as unnatural, they do have a benefit to the environment because a shorter lifespan means the cattle require less food and emit less greenhouse gas. On the other hand, the use of HGPs is another input for beef production when the world is thinking about how to use fewer, and grow our food more naturally and sustainably. The rise in demand for organic beef bears this out. There is also the issue of hormones excreted in cattle urine entering the ecosystem—the same criticism is levelled at women taking the contraceptive pill. The urine from cattle and humans enters waterways and can affect the life cycle of aquatic animals such as fish.

KEY INFO The majority of scientists around the world agree hormonal growth promotants (HGPs) used in beef cattle produce meat that is safe to eat. Some disagree.

LONG STORY SHORT Although the majority of scientific evidence supports the safety of HGPs, consumers don't like the idea of them and the European Food Safety Authority (EFSA) still bans them, citing 'concerns about possible health risks'. This has caused an ongoing international trade argument. They have positive and negative environmental impacts.

HUNGRY FOR MORE? See www.efsa.europa.eu (search for 'hormone') and www.fda.gov ('hormonal growth'). Also www.thebeefsite. com/articles/1734/the-big-question-over-beef-hormones (international beef cattle industry site) and www.apvma.gov.au/.

⊙ Meat takes weeks to digest

This old myth took hold when the bestselling (but completely unscientific) US diet book *Fit for Life* by Harvey and Marilyn Diamond was published in 1985. The premise of the book was that some foods should not be eaten together (combined). One particular dietary rule was that fruit could not be consumed at the same time as meat because meat was slower to digest and would block the digestion of the fruit causing it to 'ferment' in the stomach.

This is complete nonsense. It hasn't stopped me enjoying duck à l'orange, turkey with cranberry sauce, apricot chicken or roast beef with fruit chutney but it has caused anxiety and inconvenience for many followers of the diet. (Which makes me think, could you sue a stupid diet book for loss of enjoyment? Food for thought ...)

How is meat digested?

When it comes to digestion, meat is actually quite easy because it has no dietary fibre that requires the cooperation of bacteria in the large bowel. Digestion starts in the mouth with chewing, and human teeth are well designed for cutting (biting) and chewing meat. The masticated food is combined with saliva when it enters the stomach, at which point it is mixed with strong acid and a protein-digesting enzyme. The acid and enzyme break down the bonds that hold proteins together. The stomach then pushes its content into the small intestine where bile from the gall bladder and digestive enzymes from the pancreas are added to further break down the food into its smallest nutrient components so they can be absorbed. As a result, meat becomes a soup of amino acids—the building blocks of proteins—which are then absorbed through the walls of the small intestine and transported in the blood to where they are needed.

How long does it take?

The time it takes to fully digest and metabolise a meal varies between individuals and according to the composition of the meal—stomach emptying takes around three hours. Hardly enough time to 'rot' in the stomach. Carbohydrates spend the least time in the stomach, and then come proteins, and it's actually fat that leaves the stomach last. It takes a further three to five hours for the nutrients to be absorbed from food in the small intestine, and the longest time is required for the remnants in the large bowel where water and minerals are absorbed and bacteria work to break down the dietary fibre. The entire process to this point takes about 24 hours; however, the time it takes from eating food to flushing the waste down the toilet can be up to three days, depending on the individual and the type of food eaten. Eating more dietary fibre speeds things up.

KEY INFO Meat is fully digested by enzymes in the stomach and absorbed in the small intestine.

LONG STORY SHORT Food (including meat) takes about three hours to leave the stomach and from one to three days to be fully digested and the waste excreted.

HUNGRY FOR MORE? See www.gutfoundation.com and http://digestive.niddk.gov/ddiseases/pubs/yrdd (National Digestive Diseases Information Clearinghouse) and www.quackwatch.org/11Ind/fitforlife.html.

⊙ You can catch bird flu from chicken and swine flu from eating pork

You catch avian influenza (bird flu, or H5N1) from being in contact with live birds. Most human infections have occurred in south-east Asia where chickens roam freely in rural villages. There have also been infections reported in Europe, Turkey, Azerbaijan, Egypt and Africa. The World Health Organisation says you can't catch bird flu from eating properly cooked chicken even if it does contain the virus because the cooking kills it. The US Centers for Disease Control & Prevention (CDC) agree you can't catch it from properly handled chicken meat or eggs.

'Properly cooked' means no pink bits, and heated to an internal temperature of at least 65°C (149°F). Fortunately we don't eat chicken on the pink side because of the risk of catching other food-borne illnesses caused by *Salmonella* and *Campylobacter* and the like. Chicken is generally regarded as a 'high risk' food that requires special care to keep it safe. In any case, there is no bird flu in the UK, Europe, the USA, Canada, Australia and New Zealand and most fresh chicken meat is locally grown rather than imported. Countries the world over are on the lookout for bird flu and will pounce on it with tough bio-security measures if it appears. Citizen misunderstandings about chicken safety have already cost the poultry industry mega-bucks and it's in their interest to keep their flocks clean.

Swine flu is a virus called H1N1 that infects pigs. It rarely infects humans but transmission occurs between live pigs and people who work around them, and then from person to person like regular human flu viruses. In any case, just as you can't catch bird flu from eating chicken, you can't catch swine flu from eating pork. Cooking pork properly—to an internal temperature of 70°C (160°F)—kills viruses as well as bacteria. Australia's pig farms are free of swine flu and all fresh pork sold in Australia is home-grown. In 2010 the World Health Organisation said we were in the post-pandemic period (the worst is over) but still there have been infections reported in the USA since.

In any case, if you caught bird flu or swine flu from animals or an infected person, you wouldn't know the difference to a regular human flu. The serious danger to health from flu viruses of any kind is in vulnerable people such as the elderly and those who are already sick with low immunity.

Key info Bird flu and swine flu rarely infect people but transmission is from animals and infected people, not from food. The heat of cooking destroys viruses.

Long story short Chicken and swine flu are not common and the chicken and pork industries work very hard to prevent and eradicate viral illness. You can't catch bird flu or swine flu from eating properly cooked chicken or pork.

Hungry for more? Visit www.avianinfluenzainfo.com and www.who.int/csr/disease/avian_influenza www.who.int/csr/disease/swineflu/en and www.cdc.gov/flu/swineflu/key_facts

Chocolate

Chocolate is a legendary food: highly pleasurable but rife with mythology. Unfortunately, guilt is often associated with pleasure, and chocolate has attracted more than its fair share of guilt. The good news for chocolate lovers is not everything pleasurable is bad for you! The antioxidants in chocolate have been shown to reduce blood pressure, improve blood vessel elasticity and reduce oxidation of cholesterol. Don't read this as endorsement of chocolate as a health food, but simply as support that it is not evil and as a reason to be choosier with your chocolate. When it comes to chocolate, quality counts. It's a food best enjoyed in moderation so go for quality rather than quantity, and choose dark chocolate for its higher antioxidant content and more intense taste (which makes it harder to overeat).

⊙ Chocolate causes acne

Interestingly, acne is a problem of western civilisation—it does not exist in traditional hunter-gatherer societies. This suggests that something about our lifestyle increases the risk, but it is not entirely clear what this thing is. A poor diet can certainly show in the appearance of the skin; however, to demonise chocolate as a culprit is unfair. Acne is more related to genetics and hormones than food. Pimples form when the hair follicle becomes blocked with sebum produced by the sebaceous glands and becomes infected with bacteria. In severe cases, inflammation, nodules and cysts can form. Sex hormones can increase sebum production (thus the high prevalence of acne during puberty), and insulin can make inflammation worse.

Emerging research suggests a low-glycemic index (GI) diet can help. A small study from Melbourne published in the *American Journal of Clinical Nutrition* trialled a higher protein, lower GI diet on teenage boys with acne and found a 50 per cent improvement in lesions and inflammation. This dietary approach improved insulin sensitivity as well as reduced the acne. Although it is not proven, the reason this diet works may be because it reduced surplus insulin levels (hyperinsulineima). The boys in the study ate better in general and were also under the supervision of a dietitian. So rather than chocolate 'causing' acne, it looks like fluffy white bread, highly processed breakfast cereals and other high-GI foods may be more to blame. In fact, chocolate has a low GI.

The form of the chocolate you eat may be important in its overall effects on health and wellbeing. A little dark chocolate could be great for your skin because of its high levels of natural antioxidants, which boost blood flow to the skin and keep the skin moist and smooth. However, too many chocolate bars can displace more nutritious snacks, encourage weight gain and don't offer the antioxidants. Milk chocolate contains less antioxidants and more sugar than dark chocolate, and white chocolate is not technically chocolate at all because it contains no cocoa solids and no antioxidants. Chocolate still is—and always will be—a sometimes food to be enjoyed in moderation.

KEY INFO Acne appears to be more related to sex hormones and genetics, but emerging research suggests diet may be important, possibly via its effect on insulin levels.

LONG STORY SHORT There is no evidence that chocolate causes acne. Emerging research suggests a high-GI diet may increase the risk of acne.

HUNGRY FOR MORE? See www.acne.org and www.themainmeal. com.au (search 'teenage anti-acne diet')—this is a meat industry site. See also www.dermcoll.asn.au/public and www.aad.org/ skin-conditions.

ⓘ Carob is healthier than chocolate

I'm not sure how this myth started but it was probably around the time 'alternative health' took off and 'health food stores' started appearing. There is no support for it.

Carob 'chocolate' (a misnomer) is a sweet chocolate-like treat made from carob powder instead of cocoa. Carob powder is derived from the seed pod of *Ceratonia siliqua*, a legume tree native to the Mediterranean and Middle Eastern regions. The use of carob pods dates back to ancient Egypt. They are sweet and the flour and syrup made from them are still used to make traditional foods in countries such as Turkey. The carob bean inside the pod is also known as the locust bean and is used as a thickener

NUTRIENT	MILK CHOCOLATE (100G/3½OZ)	CAROB 'CHOCOLATE' (100G/3½OZ)
energy (kJ/cals)	2150kJ/514 cal	2154kJ/515cal
protein	8.3	11.2
fat—total	27.4	33.1
fat—saturated	16.9	31
carbohydrate—total	62	44.4
carbohydrate—sugars	55.5	42.8

Source: NUTTAB database available at www.foodstandards.gov.au/consumerinformation/nuttab2010.

in food processing and manufacturing. Although its health benefits have been researched much less than those of cocoa, carob is known to contain antioxidants. But any nutrient and phytochemical content is diluted by the process of making carob 'chocolate'.

The nutritional composition of milk chocolate versus carob 'chocolate' is shown in the table above. The kilojoule content is the same, and, if anything, the carob is worse for health because it is higher in artery-clogging saturated fats, probably from the hydrogenated vegetable oil or palm oil used in making it.

KEY INFO Milk chocolate and carob 'chocolate' are made in a similar way, but carob 'chocolate' uses carob powder instead of cocoa solids.

LONG STORY SHORT Milk chocolate and carob 'chocolate' have the same kilojoule (calorie) content, but carob has double the saturated-fat content which makes it less healthy than milk chocolate.

HUNGRY FOR MORE? Don't bother.

⏵ Chocolate is addictive

Cocoa solids used to make quality chocolate do contain feel-good chemicals such as methylxanthines, biogenic amines and cannabinoid-like fatty acids. Cocoa solids contain theobromine (like that in tea) and caffeine (like that in tea and coffee). However, they are present in such small amounts they cannot cause addiction according to the strict definition.

Calling chocolate an addictive substance is off-base for a number of reasons (although this doesn't help those struggling with overeating the stuff). Firstly, the term 'addiction' refers to drugs (yes, that includes cigarettes and alcohol), not food, and is defined as strong physiological and psychological dependence. Although so-called 'chocoholics' may say they are psychologically damaged by skipping their beloved brown stuff, it is a far cry from a true addiction to alcohol or drugs.

Addiction is technically known as 'substance dependence' and the American Psychiatric Association defines it as when a person uses a substance persistently in a compulsive and repetitive way despite problems related to its use, builds up a tolerance to it and gets withdrawal symptoms when stopped: for example, when a heroin addict goes 'cold turkey'. There are no physical withdrawal symptoms from eating chocolate (apart from a bit of weight loss perhaps). The feel-good chemicals in chocolate are present in very small amounts. Eaten in modest portions, the drug-like effects are negligible. The potentially mood-altering chemicals are found in even tinier amounts in milk chocolate, yet chocoholics tend not to be too fussy about which type of chocolate they crave. It's all about the taste and the mouth-feel and psychological aspects of enjoying a treat.

Some claim chocolate's cannibinoid-like fatty acids mimic cannibinoids found in cannabis (marijuana) by activating receptors or increasing anandamide levels. Anandamide is a lipid that binds to cannabinoid receptors and mimics the psychoactive effects of the drug. In an interesting legal case in Belgium, a guy who tested positive in a routine urine test for cannabis claimed he had not ingested or smoked cannabis but eaten a large amount of chocolate, and this explained the positive drug test. Unfortunately for him, a toxicology lab ran some tests to see if this was possible—it wasn't. The cannibinoid-like substances in chocolate are not the same as cannibinoids in cannabis. So while you can be addicted to cannabis, you can't be addicted to chocolate in a similar manner.

Some people say they 'crave chocolate', but this is due more to cultural conditioning and psychological effects than physical need. We all know you can feel like chocolate even when you're not at all hungry. Chocolate tastes wonderful and can be used as a delicious distraction to emotions such as boredom or sadness, and stressful situations. But chocolate doesn't really fix the underlying problems you want distracting from.

The other aspect to consider is that chocolate is considered a 'naughty' food. Within a dieting 'all-or-nothing' mind-set, it becomes even more desirable. For people stuck in the dieting rut of depriving themselves of everything they love to eat, chocolate can take on forbidden status. And what happens when something is forbidden? You guessed it: we want it even more! Saying you are addicted to chocolate is a socially advantageous way to say you really like chocolate in a society obsessed with slim body image and weight loss. I say thumb your nose at the 'skinny is beautiful' brigade, accept yourself the way you are and enjoy chocolate in reasonable amounts without guilt. It's funny how self-acceptance leads to better self-care—including eating well and exercising.

KEY INFO Addiction or substance abuse relates to drugs rather than food and 'chocoholism' does not meet the criteria.

LONG STORY SHORT We eat chocolate because it tastes good, and for emotional and behavioural reasons rather than physical dependence.

HUNGRY FOR MORE? See www.Allchocholate.com (chocolate company site) and www.ifnotdieting.com.au (a non-dieting approach to weight management).

⊙ Some bad foods should be avoided

The idea that 'there are no such things as bad foods, only bad diets' was once embraced by dietitians, nutritionists and the public alike, but more recently has lost its groove. I'd like to see the sentiment get its groove back. The language and rhetoric around food has taken on a good versus bad dichotomy that I don't think is healthy. Viewing some foods as inherently bad does not reflect good science or good sense, and is highly subjective. It also ignores the richness and diversity of eating experiences that enrich our lives as well as the powerful emotional connections we have with food. Consider the Christmas feast, or the breaking of the Ramadan fast, or even a slice of birthday cake. Do we really want to live in a world without cake? Is life really worth living without chocolate? Could we really dispense with the convenience of fast food in our busy lives?

Food-bashing usually comes from zealots who lack appreciation of nutrition science or the myriad of influences of food choice. I'd also suggest they have secret loves with foods they publicly denounce. I suspect many supermarket-hating wholefood crusaders love a sly jelly snake, jam doughnut, or a ... shock, horror, gasp ... chocolate cookie! I remember once having an ironic conversation with a hard-core vegetarian who felt meat was poison to his body ... while he sucked hard on a cigarette and slurred his words after one too many drinks! Human beings are an intriguing lot.

One guy who really 'walked the walk' about all foods having a place is Kansas State University Professor Mark Haub. In the tradition of Morgan Spurlock in the documentary *Super Size Me*, Haub went on a ten-week junk food diet of sweetened breakfast cereal, hot dogs, cake, muffins and cookies. He conceded to a serve of vegetables and some milk at dinner to cover his needs for vitamins and minerals. His saving grace—and the stark difference between his and Spurlock's experience—was he limited his energy intake to 7560kJ (1800 calories) a day. By contrast Spurlock deliberately overate by 'upsizing' everything. Haub's dietary experiment ended after a month and he actually lost weight. The message in this story is not to promote an all-junk-food diet but to prove a point; it's how much food you eat that matters for weight control, and perhaps the so-called 'junk food' wasn't as bad as many people expected. There is no need to banish these 'fun' foods—just enjoy them in appropriate amounts.

I think the fall from grace of 'there's no such things as bad foods, only bad diets' started when the food industry began using it as a catch-cry to market less healthy 'sometimes' foods. In an obesity epidemic of multiple causes, there is still a strong urge to lay the blame somewhere and fun foods are an easy target. While I believe wholeheartedly that 'sometimes foods' have a place in a healthy diet, I do think our food supply is weighed down with less healthy foods. Unfortunately, we like to eat fat, salt and sugar.

The solution to a healthier food supply and healthier people is not demonising food ... after all it's just food. Foods are like friends, some are great friends to see often and others are friends we see on occasion. They all have their place and are all good to have. A bit of food diplomacy may be just the thing we need to work towards a new world food order where the healthy foods have a greater say, and the 'sometimes' foods are included but not holding the balance of power.

KEY INFO Food is more than its nutritional content and adds fun and richness to life. It's not helpful to demonise individual foods.
LONG STORY SHORT All foods have a place in a healthy diet—just eat the fun food in smaller amounts and less often.
HUNGRY FOR MORE? See *Fast food and junk food cause obesity*, page 172, and visit www.choosemyplate.gov/foodgroups/ emptycalories.

⊙ Soy foods have harmful side effects

For foods that have held an important place in the diets of billions of people in Asia, soy foods have accumulated a lot of bad publicity. Soy beans are a legume very high in quality protein, with a good amount of fibre, vitamins, minerals and phytochemicals. The beans can be eaten whole, or mashed and fermented to make tempeh or miso soup paste. They can also be crushed to make soy milk, which can then be set into tofu. Processed further, soy flour or soy protein powder can also be derived and used as food ingredients.

The public doubts appear to be with a specific class of phytochemicals in soy called phytoestrogens—namely isoflavones called diadzein and genistein. Phytoestrogens are natural hormone-like substances found in some plant foods. Soy is the best known source of phytoestrogens, but they are also present in other legumes, linseeds, nuts and wholegrains. Phytoestrogens are thought to be beneficial in several ways. Firstly, eating foods containing phytoestrogens regularly is believed to reduce the risk of hormone-related cancers such as cancers of the breast and prostate. Secondly, they are thought to help reduce menopausal symptoms such as hot flushes by influencing oestrogen receptors in the body (although the evidence for this is not strong). So why are there worries about soy?

Firstly their weak oestrogen-like effects have created suspicion for the health of men and boys—would they cause feminisation or low fertility? The current evidence suggests not, but more research is needed. Soy-based formula is approved for infants by the American College of Pediatrics and UK's Department of Health (which advises consulting your GP before using), and Food Safety Australia and New Zealand (FSANZ) has found no evidence of harm from their use (and everyone knows breast feeding is best anyway). For men, numerous studies have shown regular soy intake has no effect on multiple measures of fertility (even though animal studies have shown adverse effects). Studies in China actually show men who regularly consume soy foods have a lower risk of prostate cancer.

There is also the suggestion that eating soy foods disrupts thyroid function and increases the risk of goitre (swelling of the thyroid gland and neck). Problems with foods containing naturally occurring goitrogens (substances that suppress the thyroid gland), including soy, cabbage, broccoli and cauliflower, only occur when very large quantities are consumed at the same time as a diet deficient in iodine, and they go away once iodine status is improved. Goitrogens are also partly deactivated by cooking. Interestingly, a study in San Francisco found soy-eaters had a lower risk of thyroid cancer.

There is also talk about 'anti-nutrients' in soy, such as phytic acid, trypsin inhibitors, and haemagglutinin, which are said to reduce absorption of nutrients; however, this is not an issue in varied western diets. In fact, the more we find out about phytochemicals in plant foods the more it looks like these should be re-named 'pro-nutrients' because they actually have positive effects, including anti-cancer effects.

Having said all this, many of the soy foods consumed in the USA are not eaten in the traditional manner they are in Asian cuisines—fermented, which appears to make them more digestible and healthier overall. In the USA, soy is a major industrial crop and has become omnipresent throughout the food supply. Americans consume soy products in greater quantities and in a more highly processed form. It's probably prudent to choose less adulterated soy foods and enjoy them in moderation as part of a balanced diet, so as not to overdo a good thing. I suggest:

✓✓✓ **Super healthy**
  • whole soy beans, tempeh, miso (fermented soy foods)
✓✓ **Healthy**
  • tofu, soy milk

✓ **Uncertain**
  • soy protein powders, soy protein bars.

A note for women with breast cancer

Because phytoestrogens have a weak oestrogen-like effect, there is a suggestion that women with hormone-sensitive breast cancer taking oestrogen-blocking medications (eg Tamoxifen) should not consume phytoestrogens in case they stimulate cancer growth. However, this has only been demonstrated in test-tube and animal studies. Cancer experts suggest it's OK for breast cancer survivors to consume soy foods in moderation, but caution against the use of phytoestrogen supplements from any source. More research is needed to determine if phytoestrogen supplements have a protective or an adverse effect.

KEY INFO Soy foods contain naturally occurring phytoestrogens (isoflavones) which exert very weak oestrogen-like effects; these appear to protect against hormone-related cancers in men and women. The isoflavones also have weak effects on thyroid function that only cause problems when a person is iodine-deficient.

LONG STORY SHORT Soy beans are highly nutritious and rich in quality protein. The more they are processed, the less they are likely to exert health benefits. Enjoy soy foods such as whole soy beans, tempeh, tofu and soy milk in moderation and give highly processed soy protein powders a miss.

HUNGRY FOR MORE? Soy Connection newsletter—www.talksoy. com—written by independent health experts (and funded by US soybean farmers). The Soy Story—www.soyfacts.com.au— from Sanitarium, marketers of vegetarian foods. including soy foods endorsed by ISAB (International Soy Advisory Board).

⏵ Potatoes are bad for you

The poor old potato is a much maligned food but it really doesn't deserve all the criticism. It has been called fattening, bad for blood sugars, and generally undesirable, but this really isn't fair. Spud-lovers can relax. Potatoes are good for you.

Potatoes are starchy tubers that grow underground. I remember as a child digging them out of the soil and roasting them whole in an open fire at a friend's farm—pure joy! They are high in carbohydrates for energy and stimulate that feel-good brain chemical called serotonin. Eating potatoes helps you feel that life is good. Potatoes are also a good source of vitamin C and fibre (especially if you eat the skin) and also contain vitamin B6 and potassium.

People often say potatoes are fattening, but this is an exaggeration. Any food containing kilojoules can be fattening if you eat too much, and carbohydrate in potatoes is no more or less fattening than kilojoules from any other source. It is sad for low-carb diets to recommend followers eat mashed cauliflower and pretend it's potato. Just enjoy a bit of both.

Eaten whole with minimal additions, potatoes are difficult to overeat due to their high 'satiety index'. Boiled potatoes are one of the most filling foods you can eat. Potatoes cut into French fries and cooked in unhealthy fats are a different story, but don't tar all potatoes with the same fast-food brush. If you are a French-fry (hot chip) fan, then look for establishments that cook them in healthy oil, keep your portions small and skip the salt. This way, you can have your chip and eat it.

Most potatoes have a high GI but even GI queen, Professor Jennie Brand Miller, agrees there is no need to ban high-GI foods altogether. Just enjoy them in a balanced meal with plenty of other vegetables and some lean protein. There are also lower GI varieties such as canned new potatoes (GI 65), and the newer Nadine (GI 57), Nicola (GI 58) and Carisma (GI 55). Sweet potato has a GI of 61. Adding a little healthy fat also lowers the GI, so in fact nice fat potato wedges roasted in some olive, sunflower or canola oil are a healthy, lower GI option. Adding vinegar also lowers the glycemic response. To keep potatoes healthy, avoid serving them with butter, cream and/or cheese.

One of the things I love about the potato, apart from its gorgeous taste and texture, is how simple it is to prepare. I simply wash, cut and microwave on high (or steam) until tender, and lightly dress with some extra virgin olive oil, dried rosemary and black pepper. Use whatever healthy oils, herbs and spices you like for an instant accompaniment to lean meat, chicken or fish and steamed greens. And a good tip: always cook more than you need because cooled and reheated potato contains a beneficial kind of dietary fibre called resistant starch that keeps your bowel healthy. That's what I call potato magic.

KEY INFO Potatoes have nutritional goodies such as fibre, vitamin C, B6 and potassium. Although many have a high GI, this doesn't mean you shouldn't eat them.

LONG STORY SHORT Enjoy potatoes in moderation as part of a balanced meal and prepared in healthy ways. French fries are not the best way to enjoy the health benefits!

HUNGRY FOR MORE? See www.potatomuseum.com and www. glycemicindex.com.

⊙ Wheat is hard to digest and makes you bloated

The idea that wheat is somehow bad and causes bloating and other vague symptoms is a modern one. It is perpetuated in an environment of high stress, eating excess, too much choice and a complex and challenging food environment. People with coeliac disease can't tolerate the gluten in wheat, but gluten is also in rye, barley and oats. Wheat contains fructans that upset the bowels of those with fructose intolerance (a new area of nutrition research)—however, this only affects a small percentage of people. Interestingly, anti-wheat sentiments have spread beyond those in the food intolerance community.

Wheat has been eaten for thousands of years and is still a staple food around the world. Think of the huge varieties of different breads from multicultural cuisines, as well as pasta, couscous and noodles. Its cultivation allowed humankind to shift from hunting and gathering to living in settlements far and wide with a steady supply of food.

Wheat is not particularly hard for healthy people to digest. If it were, humans would not have flourished and populated the world while eating it. Its high protein content compared with other widely cultivated grains such as corn and rice give it a distinct advantage for human health. Wheat is composed mostly of starch (carbohydrate), but with a good amount of protein (gluten) and some good fats (germ) and fibre (husk). The higher fibre and nutrient content of wholegrain wheat (in wholegrain and wholemeal foods) actually promotes digestive health and reduces the risk of chronic diseases such as heart disease and bowel cancer.

Intestinal bloating is caused by intestinal gas. It is more common in women, is closely related to constipation and has multiple causes, including insufficient fibre, food intolerance or simply not being able to release gas when necessary (for physiological and social reasons, such as sharing an office!). If farting in public were more acceptable, bloating would be far less of a problem. The fact is healthy food with fibre makes you fart—end of story. It's not an illness or a physical problem: it's normal. In some women, however, there may be some miscoordination of the lower bowel which makes releasing gas more difficult.

Many people find gradually increasing the fibre in their diet helpful for reducing 'the bloat', and most people do not consume the target amounts: 38g (1^{1}/$_{3}$oz) a day for men and 28g (1oz) a day for women. It is important to increase fibre gradually to give the body time to adjust.

Food intolerance can cause uncomfortable bowel symptoms, including bloating, but these can be due to a myriad of causes that have nothing to do with wheat—for example, lactose in milk, glutamates in tomatoes and parmesan, salicyclates in capsicum (sweet peppers), chillies and herbs, and amines in canned tuna, bacon, cheese and chocolate. An 'elimination diet and re-challenge' under the supervision of an experienced dietitian (RD or APD) is the gold standard diagnosis method—blood tests are invalid.

One criticism of the modern western diet is a lack of variety. Because of the dominance of a handful of major crops—including wheat, corn, soybeans and rice—in intensive agriculture, wheat tends to be overrepresented in our food supply. It's too easy to eat wheat cereal for breakfast, wheat bread for lunch and pasta for dinner: the same staple thrice daily. If there is any sensitivity to wheat, it's more likely to rear its ugly head in this excessive consumption scenario. For a happier tummy and for nutritional reasons, it's good to vary grains within the day and from day to day.

Key info There's nothing difficult to digest about wheat: it is a dietary staple around the world. Modern western diets contain a lot of wheat and if bloating is a problem, increasing variety is a good idea. Bloating can be caused by food intolerance to a number of natural food components including gluten, lactose, amines, salicylates, glutamates or fructans (and only fructans are found in wheat).

LONG STORY SHORT We should all aim to eat a variety of grains and preferably wholegrain versions.

HUNGRY FOR MORE? See www.allaboutwheat.info and www. sswahs.nsw.gov.au/rpa/allergy.

⊙ Coca Cola can be used as a household cleanser

Although a glass of Coke may leave your mouth with a nice clean feeling after eating a slice of cheesy pizza, it's approved 'food acid 338' that does the trick here. Not the (not-for-human-consumption) detergents, solvents, fragrance, ammonia, dye, and alcohol you get in a handy multi-surface cleanser.

According to the ingredient label (where they are listed in descending order), regular Coca Cola is carbonated purified water, cane sugar, caramel 150d (a food colouring, also known as sulfite ammonia caramel, acid-proof caramel, soft-drink caramel), food acid 338 (phosphoric acid), a flavour (the mystery ingredient) and caffeine with 'no added preservatives or artificial flavours'. Some of these ingredients may not sound like something you want inside you—but you'll find them in many foods and beverages including all the other brands of cola.

Coke and other soft drinks don't cause kidney stones either. The biggest risk factor for kidney stones is dehydration. Kidney stones are quite common, tend to run in families, can form when your urine contains too much of certain substances (there are different types) and can recur (meaning that if you have had them once it's likely you'll get them again).

Key info People have been enjoying Coca Cola for around 125 years in one formulation or another. It has been under the food safety authority microscope on a number of occasions. The main problem with Coke and other soft drinks is that they are packed with sugar and, if you overdo it, it helps you pile on the kilos. Say no thanks to the daily soft drink fix or jumbo container and if weight's a problem, opt for the diet varieties—a regular 375ml (12fl oz) can of any brand of cola (like other soft drinks) has 8–10 teaspoons sugar.

Long story short This myth is essentially a version of the Coke dissolves teeth, nails, coins, steaks etc. myths. Have you noticed that there are many myths about Coca Cola and few about other cola brands? This is one of those facts that should sound some alarm bells. The downside of being a leading brand like Coca Cola, is that lots of people love to hate you and thanks to the internet, they have a forum for going viral.

HUNGRY FOR MORE? There are some great websites where you can quickly check out the 'legit status' of the latest food myth to pop up in your inbox. My favourite is snopes.com, the definitive internet reference source for urban legends, folklore, myths, rumours, and misinformation.

⊙ Gluten-free diets are better for you

For some people this is absolutely true. If you have coeliac disease or a gluten-sensitive chronic skin condition called dermatitis herpetiformis (DH), a gluten-free diet is a lifesaver. And it's for life.

Gluten can also be a trigger of gut symptoms, bloating and tiredness in some people (who don't have coeliac disease). Recent research published in the *American Journal of Gastroenterology* is showing that people with irritable bowel syndrome, for example, can benefit from a gluten-free or reduced-gluten diet.

For the rest of us, the answer is no, gluten-free diets are not better for you.

'Gluten-free' isn't a magic bullet to a better diet, nor is it code for 'healthy eating' or an easy way to achieve weight loss. But going gluten-free has become a health fad. The problem is that it's not an easy diet to manage and if not well planned you can end up with an unbalanced, unhealthy diet low in wholegrains (and all their nutritional goodies such as B vitamins) and fibre and high in fat and added sugar (which is what's in many of the highly processed gluten-free foods on supermarket shelves, especially in the sweet biscuit, bar and cake category). Few products are based on wholegrain versions of gluten-free grains, even though they are healthier.

If you ask people who have to eat this way they will often report that their diet lacks variety (the list of what's out is a very long one) and that they feel hungry all the time and run out of energy throughout the day because those slowly digested starchy staples—like grainy breads, pasta, muesli and porridge oats—are off the menu. It also seems that going gluten-free can reduce your friendly gut bacteria and immune function. And doing it properly can be hard—hard to shop for, stick to and feed the family (think of making two meals every night).

It doesn't make sense that wheat (the most common source of gluten in our diet), barley, oats and rye would somehow be

What is coeliac disease?

Coeliac disease is the most common and one of the most under-diagnosed hereditary autoimmune diseases and it is caused by an intolerance to gluten. It tends to run in families and mainly affects people of European origin. It's not just a childhood problem. Coeliac disease affects those of any age. Symptoms include abdominal pain, diarrhoea, lethargy and iron deficiency.

In Britain, Australia and New Zealand, coeliac disease affects up to one in every 100 people; in the USA the rate is lower, about one in 133 people. On top of this, for every person diagnosed with coeliac disease, there's likely to be another eight or nine with symptoms or complications attributable to it.

If you have coeliac disease and you eat something that contains gluten, you will get an immune reaction in your small intestine. This damages your intestinal wall, reducing its ability to absorb nutrients from food and leading to deficiencies of the essential vitamins and minerals that your body needs for growth, health, healing and energy.

If it's not diagnosed and treated, coeliac disease can affect children's growth and development. In adults, it can lead to long-term health problems, including osteoporosis (due to calcium malabsorption), infertility, miscarriage, tooth decay and an increased risk of cancers of the digestive system.

It never goes away.

The good news is that you don't need drugs to deal with it. You can manage the disease effectively by following a strict gluten-free diet. By doing this, your intestinal wall will heal so nutrients can be absorbed, your symptoms will be resolved and this can help prevent long-term health problems.

---

harmful. These grains have been cultivated for thousands of years and used to make a huge range of staple foods, including leavened bread, flat breads, pasta, noodles and porridge. It would be very hard to feed everyone on planet Earth without them.

KEY INFO Some people need to follow a gluten-free (or reduced gluten) diet, but most of us don't. Don't listen to what the people in the local organic store or café or helping in your school canteen tell you. Word of mouth is notoriously unreliable. More importantly, don't self-diagnose and put yourself on a gluten-free diet. The worst thing you can do is start following a gluten-free diet before you have a diagnosis of coeliac disease because this can prevent a correct diagnosis being made.

LONG STORY SHORT If you suspect food is somehow the cause of your tummy troubles or tiredness, see your doctor for a definitive diagnosis through blood test and intestinal biopsy. If your symptoms are not due to coeliac disease, see a registered dietitian with experience in food intolerance to help you identify the real problem and put together a healthy balanced diet that's right for you.

HUNGRY FOR MORE? See www.coeliac.org.uk; www.celiac.org; www.coeliac.org.au, and www.coeliac.co.nz.

▶ White foods have little nutritional value

It would be nice if there were a simple colour rule for healthy eating. But there isn't. This rule seems to have come about to discourage consumption/over-consumption of sugar, salt and white flour. But brown sugar is on a par with white in the 'little nutritional value' stakes, and pink salt matches white for sodium, gram for gram.

When it comes to grains, white rice and white pasta are important food staples around the world providing energy, vitamins, minerals and even a little protein, but they do have something missing—they have been refined and in the process lost some of their nutritional goodness. For example, white bread and flour have no bran or germ as a result. Choosing 'brown' or wholegrain versions of popular staples such as bread, rice and pasta delivers important extra benefits in terms of fibre and B vitamins.

Key info If you have a sweet tooth, keep your added sugar intake (brown or white) moderate—no more than 30g (6 teaspoons) a day. Skip salt and rev up the flavour with herbs and spices. Make sure at least half your grains come from wholegrain— traditional oats, brown rice and pasta, and wholegrain (or wholemeal) bread and cereals.

Long story short The rule was not intended to apply to white foods such as milk (chocolate milk isn't better for you), egg whites or white veggies like cauliflower or cannellini beans or new potatoes or white fish. Enjoy a balanced diet that includes a wide variety of foods of all colours, including some 'white' ones, especially fish.

Hungry for more? See *Brown sugar is healthier than white* (page 82), *Sea salt is healthier* (page 190) and *Brown eggs are healthier than white* (page 168).

⊙ Brown eggs are healthier than white

Some people choose brown eggs and some like white, but truth be told, the colour of the egg has no effect on the contents. It's just consumer preference. In general, chicken breeds with white ear lobes lay white eggs, and chickens with red ear lobes lay brown eggs (but even this isn't a hard and fast rule). And of course, once you peel or crack the egg, they are all the same inside.

Brown or white, eggs are a highly nutritious and versatile food. They contain perfect protein—just the right balance of amino acids our body needs. They are also packed with vitamins and minerals such as vitamin A, E, folate and B12, antioxidants lutein and zeaxanthin that help maintain healthy eyes, and also long-chain omega-3 fats (like the ones in fish). A typical 50g (1¾oz) egg contains 5g fat, of which only 1.5g is saturated. The common belief that eggs cause high cholesterol is untrue. This idea was made on the assumption that cholesterol in food became cholesterol in your blood, which we now know to be incorrect.

But some eggs do have eggstra benefits.

Omega-3 enriched eggs are produced by providing hens with linseed- (flaxseed) enriched feed, which is naturally rich in alpha-linolenic acid (omega-3 fat). Studies have shown that eating them has positive effects on our blood fats: higher good (HDL) cholesterol and lower triglyceride levels. Omega-3 enriched eggs are also one of the few foods that contain long-chain omega-3 fatty acids (DHA and EPA), which we normally get from eating fish, and so they are great for vegetarians.

As for the difference between free-range and cage eggs, there's little scientific evidence of nutritional differences to date and some good quality research is needed. However, I've noticed free-range eggs have yolk that is orangier, which signals antioxidants such as lutein and xeaxanthin. It would make sense that free-range chickens might have the opportunity to pick up many extras in their diet as they forage on greens and could transfer antioxidants from these to their eggs, but I'm not aware of any quality data to back this up.

Egg freshness is important too. Eggs will keep for up to five weeks, but their quality declines a little with time. The best way to store eggs is in the fridge in their original carton.

KEY INFO Brown or white, eggs are a highly nutritious food representing great value.

LONG STORY SHORT An egg a day (brown or white) is fine for most of us—provided it's not soaking in bacon fat or doused in cream or sitting on a piece of toast with a slab of butter.

HUNGRY FOR MORE? I hope this lays this matter to rest but if you really need eggstra info, check out www.incredibleegg.org.

▶ Tea and coffee are dehydrating

Everyone assumes that caffeine-containing beverages such as tea and coffee dehydrate, but it's an urban legend. Seriously high amounts of caffeine are needed before you lose more water than you drink in your cup of tea or coffee. Even if you had a really, really strong cup of tea or coffee, which is quite hard to make, you would still have a net gain of fluid.

So the good news is that enjoying tea and coffee in moderation does contribute to your daily fluid quota. Dehydration is more likely if caffeine is taken in tablet form.

What's moderation? For tea it's around three to four cups a day. For coffee it's around two to three cups of brewed coffee; if you have high blood pressure, cut that back to one to two cups. The key thing with coffee is to resist temptation to upsize. Use a regular cup and order regular-sized servings. If you make your own, use the single shot function on your espresso machine.

Pregnant women and older children should try to stick to one to two cups of weak coffee or tea a day.

With tea and coffee watch the extras—the milk, sugar and biscuits or cake! Opt for low-fat milk and if you need the drink sweetened, add a little sugar, gradually using less—you may find you even prefer it without after a while.

Key info Tea and coffee are a source of essential fluids, as well as protective antioxidants that help look after heart and blood vessels. They are also social drinks that bring us together and help us take time out. It makes sense to avoid caffeine drinks at night if you have trouble sleeping.

Long story short For good health you should drink plenty of water, but tea and coffee (in moderation) do count toward your total daily fluid intake. Water is essentially replacing fluid. Tea and coffee replace fluids and contain antioxidants, so they've got two things going for them.

Hungry for more? See www.liptont.com/tea_health/beverage_guide (tea company site, based on a scientific publication) and www.coffee-tea.co.uk.

The amount of caffeine in tea and coffee

The amount depends on the brand and type and how strong you make it. Here's a rough guide.

1 CUP (250ML/8FL OZ)	CAFFEINE (MG)
tea	10–50
decaf instant coffee	3
decaf percolated	5–8
decaf espresso (per 30ml/1 oz shot)	5–8
instant coffee	60–80
percolated/plunger coffee	60–120

▶ Fast food and junk food cause obesity

Excess body fat is simply stored kilojoules you haven't used. And as far as your body is concerned, one kilojoule is pretty much like another no matter where it comes from—fast food or healthy food. The body stores leftovers because in the past stocking up on food like this was the key to surviving times when food was scarce.

To prove that, in weighty matters, kilojoule counting is more important than the nutritional quality, Kansas State University human nutrition professor Mark Haub became a guinea pig for his students while teaching a course on energy balance, putting himself on a ten-week 'junk food' diet (see a day on Mark's junk diet, opposite). He also took a multivitamin pill and drank a protein shake every day, munched on some veggies and reduced his food intake from around 11,000 kilojoules (2630 calories) a day to around 7500 kilojoules (1800 calories). He lost 12kg (26½lb).

Haub makes that point that in his own case that when he was eating 'healthy', he wasn't 'healthier' because he was eating too much and was overweight. He showed you can eat too much of the good things.

KEY INFO It's kilojoules **in** and kilojoules **out** that count. Our bodies constantly burn kilojoules to keep us going. Once the daily business of breathing, eating, moving and other activities are met, any unused or surplus kilojoules get stored, mostly in the form of fat. This means if you take in more than you use you will gain weight. Look at it like this: kilojoules are the ultimate policeman of fat, refined starch and sugar content.

LONG STORY SHORT When it comes to the cause of obesity, eating more kilojoules than you use and being inactive are the big problems for most people today. But your genes play a part too. Some people are genetically programmed to be larger and the effort to slim down substantially is unrealistic. If this is you, be as healthy as you can. You are better off being fat and enjoying a healthy diet than being fat and eating badly. The same goes for physical activity—you are better off being fat and fit, than a fat couch potato.

HUNGRY FOR MORE? See www.iaso.org/iotf for information on obesity.

What Mark Haub ate

On 10 September 2010 (according to his Facebook page), his diet consisted of:

- a double espresso
- two servings of Hostess Twinkies Golden Sponge Cake
- one Centrum Advance Formula 'From A To Zinc' pill
- one serving of Little Debbie Star Crunch cookies
- a Diet Mr Dew drink
- half a serving of Doritos Cool Ranch corn chips
- two servings of Kellogg's Corn Pops cereal
- a serving of whole milk
- half a serving of raw baby carrots
- one and a half servings of Duncan Hines Family Style Chewy Fudge brownie
- half a serving of Little Debbie Zebra Cake
- one serving of Muscle Milk Protein Shake drink

TOTAL: 6674kJ (1589 calories)

▶ Nutrition labelling on fast food improves choices

Keep in mind the old saying: 'You can lead a horse to water, but you can't make him drink.'

Information may be empowering but, when it comes to what we eat, it only goes so far. We are apparently helpless to take meaningful action when tastebuds rule. For example, when US researchers compared fast food purchases in New York City (with calorie counts prominently displayed on menus) and neighbouring Newark (no calorie counts at all), they found the calorie content of what customers bought was the same in both cities. This, despite the fact that 28 per cent of the New Yorkers said the calorie counts had influenced them to order better—a classic case of saying one thing and doing another. Worthy of note is that the stores were in poor neighbourhoods. Could it be that the socially disadvantaged benefit less from the 'information is power' approach?

I certainly support knowledge to empower people to choose healthier food, but should it be so hard and in such small print on the back of the pack? Currently, there's a push to introduce front-of-pack traffic lights to make it all easier. I understand why many people find this so appealing. They stand out. They are easy to read. A real no-brainer. Buy green not red. Or be an amber gambler …

However, the traffic light system aims to make something very complex into something very simple, and we lose a lot in the translation.

- What about highly nutritious foods rich in good fats from nuts, avocados, seeds and olive oil? Will these attract a big fat red spot despite their obvious health benefits?
- What about puffed-up, high-GI, alternatively sweetened, refined cereal products? Will these get the green light when they are a nutritionally poorer choice?

When nutrition labelling led us down the garden path: the sorry low-fat saga

We all want life and the daily choices we make shopping to be simple. But that's not going to happen—certainly not in the supermarket. Life isn't simple, nor is the best nutrition science. Things change. New discoveries are made and sometimes they tell us that yesterday's villain may not be quite such a bad guy after all. The low-fat story is a good example of this. We now know that it's not how much fat you eat, it's the type of fat that counts. It's fair to say that many people are scared of fat these days and try to avoid it (see *Low-fat diet is best*, page 35).

Reducing the complexity of food down to three adverse nutrients is missing the forest for the trees, and without solid evidence that it will make any difference to public health or your health. Australian researchers measured how consumers responded to red/amber/green traffic light labels and found they made no difference to purchasing decisions.

Another question about the effectiveness of nutrition labelling: do people really care whether fast food is healthy or not? The majority of people (72%) in the New York study didn't. Or do people purchase for other reasons, such as taste, price and convenience?

Young men are big consumers of fast food and well known for their risk-taking behaviour. I've heard stories of young men daring each other to eat the unhealthiest item on fast food menus, and gaining the respect of their peers when they manage to stuff down two or three ... plus dessert! Some socially unaware fast food companies depend on such 'extreme-eating'. You know, the ones that have 72oz (2kg) steaks on the menu: free to those who can finish it. Obscene.

Key info Knowledge can be power, but it's up to us to use it.
Long story short Knowledge doesn't always lead to behavious change. Nutrition labelling has been on the back of packaged foods for years, but we are just getting fatter. There's no new labelling silver bullet such as 'traffic lights' that's going to solve obesity and other related health problems and save governments billions in health care costs. What we do need are public education campaigns, cooking classes in schools and reasonable nutritional standards for fast foods.
Hungry for more? Search for 'calorie labelling for fast food' to see what's happening in your area.

PART 3

In sickness and health

It was the ancient Greek physician Hippocrates who said, 'Let food be thy medicine and medicine be thy food'. As a rule for healthy living it has stood up well to the test of time. I'm a big believer in the power of food to keep us healthy and cure what ails us but only when there is good evidence for it. There are so many crazy rules, marketing promises and food fads: why make eating and drinking more difficult or expensive when there is no real benefit?

⏵ Cravings tell us what our body needs

Some people—especially women—say they eat what they crave because their 'body knows best'. However, the most common food craving in women is chocolate—a food the body doesn't need at all (see *Chocolate is addictive*, page 149). Unsurprisingly, cravings for broccoli, eggs and green leafy vegetables are rare. In fact, cravings are more common in women than in men and the facts point to the mind and not the body calling the shots. Sweet cravings can fluctuate throughout a woman's menstrual cycle, indicating hormones play a role. But I've never seen a premenstrual woman crave a bowl of oats that would best meet her need for slow-release carbs. Brain imaging studies have found men are more able to resist food urges than women, and are better able to switch off the signals from the brain that say 'eat chocolate now'.

For some people feeling low, food cravings may be an attempt to prop up serotonin levels—which is akin to self-medicating with food. However, it is non-physiological factors that guide them toward sweets and cakes because they would achieve a good serotonin boost with the carbohydrate in a glass of milk or a slice of toast.

We're hard-wired to eat a variety of foods to ensure our nutrient needs are met. In one way, wanting something different to eat is the body's way of getting what it needs. But cravings for cookies, ice cream and chocolate all point to a desire for pleasure rather than nutrients. Food cravings are most often for 'naughty' foods and prohibition simply leads to greater desire. If food cravings are problematic, psychological help is needed. In one study, visually picturing something that is non-food related was able to reduce the grip of food cravings.

It is common for women to experience both food aversions and food cravings during pregnancy but research is sketchy as to why. While people joke about women craving pickles and ice cream, more typical cravings are for sweet, salty or sour foods. Although hormonal upheaval is blamed, there's no good science to support the idea that women crave food they need more of. Weirdly, some women crave inedible things like dirt, clay and even cigarette butts (eeuw): this is called pica.

By the way, in food intolerance circles it is common for patients to 'crave' foods they are intolerant to, even when the foods they crave cause them to feel unwell.

KEY INFO Cravings are usually for less healthy, high kilojoule (calorie) foods. Cravings are 'in the mind' not the body.
LONG STORY SHORT Indulge your desire for less healthy foods in moderation. You have a large brain to think through what's best to eat. If you're feeling low, try regular meals including low GI carbs and protein to balance serotonin levels and regulate mood.
HUNGRY FOR MORE? See www.psychologicalscience.org/index.php/news/releases/the-psychology-of-food-cravings.

▶ Everyone should drink eight glasses of water a day

Most adults need around 2–2.5 litres (4–5 pints) of fluid daily but not all this needs to be water. Fluid needs vary greatly, according to climate, physical activity, body size, diet and state of health.

Eight glasses of water a day is eight metric cups (8 x 8oz glasses) or 2 litres. Some experts say there is absolutely no scientific foundation for this oft-given advice. This puzzled me because I thought there were principles and guidelines to calculate a person's fluid requirements and they roughly equate to this eight-glass rule of thumb. Are these guidelines I've been using based on good scientific evidence? Before you throw your water bottle against the nearest brick wall, here's more information to 'fill out' the story of how much water we should drink.

Everyone knows we can't survive long without water. For the more morbid among you, survival time is around one week but can be as little as a few hours for a marathon runner experiencing catastrophic heatstroke. Water is essential for life and is needed for temperature regulation, digestion, metabolism, absorption of nutrients and excretion of waste. About half the water needed each day goes to sweat and water vapour in our breath. Water accounts for 50 to 80 per cent of our lean body mass (men have slightly more than women), and the proportion goes down as we age. Replacement of lost water is vital to maintain normal functioning.

The reference values used in the UK, Europe, USA, Australia and New Zealand acknowledge it is difficult to experimentally derive Estimated Average Requirements (EAR) for water because of individual variation. Because of this, they give an Adequate Intake (AI) based on the median intake of the population. This is a roundabout way of saying they came up with a best guess: around 2 litres/64fl oz (8 cups) for women and 2.5 litres/80fl oz (10 cups) for men, with clear caveats that people living in hot climates or who are very physically active need more. You can see how the eight-glass a day rule is starting to sound plausible. No

Upper Limit (UL) has been set because over-hydration causing hyponatremia (dangerously low electrolyte sodium levels) is unlikely in normal circumstances.

The eight-glass rule fails to recognise there is a lot of water already in food, especially fruits and vegetables, as well as the obvious liquid and semi-solid foods such as soups, yoghurt and custard. Typically, the intrinsic water in food contributes 2¾ to 3¼ cups per day. Water is also a byproduct of metabolism: around 1 cup per day is produced this way. So more accurately, the eight-glass a day rule should be more like four to six.

What about thirst?

I've heard the human thirst mechanism is a poor indicator of fluid needs and we should drink even when we aren't thirsty, but is this true? The scientific literature suggests this is only true in athletes, because their fluid needs are high, and the elderly, because their thirst mechanism is poor. For the rest of us, our thirst serves us well.

So, drink when you feel thirsty and don't feel you have to gulp down eight glasses of water a day. For many, four to six glasses is probably enough. And remember tea, milk, juice and coffee all contribute valuable fluids—just go easy on the sweetened drinks to prevent kilojoule/calorie blow-outs.

KEY INFO Many people don't need to drink eight glasses of water a day, but fluid needs vary a lot. We get some fluid from the foods we eat and some is produced in the body as part of metabolism.
LONG STORY SHORT Drink when you feel thirsty, and drink more during exercise and in hot weather. Water is a good drink but fluid needs can also be met by tea, weak coffee, milk and juice.
HUNGRY FOR MORE? Go to http://fnic.nal.usda.gov and search for 'Water and fluid needs'

▶ Saturated fats aren't that bad

The World Heart Federation says, 'A diet high in saturated fat increases the risk of heart disease ... It is estimated to cause about 31% of coronary heart disease worldwide.' The Heart Foundation (Australia) reviewed the evidence about dietary fats and heart health and concluded the following:

1. Saturated fat intake is associated with Coronary Heart Disease (CHD)—that is, saturated fats are bad for your heart.
2. Replacing saturated fat with unsaturated fats has a greater positive influence on CHD risk than replacing saturated fat with carbohydrates—in other words, replace bad fats with good fats, don't follow a fat-free diet.
3. Increasing saturated fat results in an increase in total and LDL (bad) cholesterol compared with carbohydrates and unsaturated fats—that is, eating too many saturated fats will raise your cholesterol.
4. Lowering dietary saturated fat to less than 7 per cent of energy intake with restricted dietary cholesterol results in further LDL (bad) cholesterol lowering than diets containing less than 10 per cent of energy intake from saturated fat. The less saturated fats you eat, the better your cholesterol will be.

A review by the best scientific brains working in the area of dietary fat and cardiovascular disease came to similar conclusions but they also said just using cholesterol level is not enough when assessing risk—we have to look at lots of factors (and good doctors calculate absolute risk for an individual based on a range of factors). The brains trust also said that the effect of particular foods cannot be predicted only on their saturated fat content—there are other nutrients at play. This leads me nicely into dairy foods.

The group most defensive about saturated fats is the dairy lobby. Although dairy foods are one of the biggest sources of saturated fats in the western diet, population studies show people who consume the most dairy tend to live longer and have a lower risk of heart disease. Perhaps dairy's bundle of other important nutrients makes up for their saturated fat? Or maybe the studies are flawed? We know the measurement of dairy food intake in populations is not perfect—for example, did people eat low-fat dairy foods? The bottom line is you don't need to throw the baby out with the bathwater—just choose low-fat dairy foods to get all of the good stuff and less of the bad. Cheese is not the healthiest dairy food choice because it is high in both saturated fat and salt, so choose low-fat milk and yoghurt on a daily basis. Of course butter is not part of the dairy group and has no redeeming nutritional qualities for its hefty whack of saturated fat—so, to be prudent, just eat very little of it (see *Butter is better than margarine because it's natural*, page 101).

It's clear we need to be replacing saturated fats with unsaturated fats, but what does this mean in food terms? It means eating less 'extra' foods such as cakes, biscuits, confectionery and pastries, and less 'fast foods' that are deep fried in unhealthy fats. If we all did this, we probably wouldn't need to worry about ensuring our meat was lean and our dairy low fat! The other issue is western diets contain relatively large amounts of animal foods, so we need to be choosier about them. And we don't eat anywhere near our quota of protective plant foods, so this also requires extra dietary caution with saturated fats

KEY INFO Studies show that saturated fats increase heart disease risk and unsaturated fats reduce it. Beneficial nutrients in some foods may help shave off some of the risk of their saturated fat content.

LONG STORY SHORT Good scientific evidence says your risk of heart disease goes down if you replace saturated fats in meat and milk fat, butter and hard cooking fats with unsaturated fats found in oils, margarine spreads, nuts, seeds and fish. It helps greatly to eat less 'extra' foods such as pastries, cakes, biscuits and deep fried fast foods.

HUNGRY FOR MORE? See www.hsph.harvard.edu/nutritionsource/ what-should-you-eat/fats-and-cholesterol.

⊙ We need to eat salt

Not to be too dramatic, but the saying 'pure, white and deadly' is quite fitting for this popular seasoning. If it's good luck you want, you're better off throwing a pinch of salt over your shoulder than into your dinner. The problem is too much salt increases blood pressure and this increases the risk of heart attack and stroke. An investigation published in the high-powered *Lancet* medical journal on the costs and benefits of population strategies to prevent chronic disease found cutting our salt intake has more potential to save lives than stopping smoking. Perhaps we need a health warning on salt as well as cigarette packets? (I can hear the howls of 'nanny state' already!)

Sodium is essential for health—without it we could not exist. It is part of the wondrous bath of fluids both inside our cells and out. We obtain enough sodium naturally in the food we eat, and our kidneys are very clever at keeping things in balance. Eating salt is a relatively new phenomenon in the evolution of humans, and in fact there are still remote hunter-gatherer tribes who do not eat salt at all and live to a ripe old age.

Salt is the everyday word for sodium chloride. We get salt from drying out lakewater or seawater, or mining it from ancient underground sea beds. It can also be chemically manufactured. In times gone by it was highly valued and used as currency, which is where the saying 'worth his/her salt' came from. Before refrigeration, salt was highly valued because of its ability to preserve food—it meant the difference between survival and starvation before the industrial revolution. Despite not needing salt to preserve our food any more, we still have the taste for it and add it in large quantities to our food. Technically speaking, some salt can enhance and balance flavours in foods but it is fair to say we've gone overboard. You can re-train you tastebuds to appreciate desalinated food by cutting down gradually over four to six weeks.

It's all salt

- Table salt is the one in most salt shakers. It is fine-ground, refined salt typically from rock salt and usually with some additives to keep it free flowing (anti-caking agents such as sodium silicoaluminate or magnesium carbonate).

- Iodised salt is table salt with a minute amount of potassium iodide, sodium iodide or iodate added. The iodine is added to help reduce the chance of iodine deficiency, which commonly leads to thyroid problems such as goitre.

- Sea salt is produced by the evaporation of seawater and comes in flakes and crystals. It usually has no additives.

- Rock salt is mined from underground deposits left behind in ancient sea beds. It is sold in coarse form with larger particles, or ground up into fine table salt.

- Kosher salt is additive-free and coarse grained.

This whole issue has been confused by the use of salt as a vehicle to add essential iodine to the diet in nations where deficiency is a problem, such as some parts of the USA, in South Africa, Australia and New Zealand. We've put ourselves in the silly position of, on the one hand, saying, 'don't add salt to food', and on the other, saying 'choose iodised salt' (because we know you use it anyway). This pragmatic solution to the iodine problem is very effective but it also smacks of hypocrisy and leaves citizens questioning the wisdom of well-meaning public health experts.

The bottom line is to use as little salt as possible. Importantly, check the label of processed foods such as bread, sauces and snacks to find the lowest in sodium—this is where the majority of the salt in our diet comes from. If you'd rather starve than cut back on salt, you're underestimating the marvellous ability of human tastebuds to adapt to less salt over time. If you reduce the salt in your diet gradually, the suffering will be minimal. Get into taste sensations offered by lemons, herbs, spices, garlic and onions and soon a whole world of real food flavours will open up.

KEY INFO Sodium is essential for life but we get enough from unprocessed food naturally. Salt is added to food for taste. The taste for salt can be unlearned.

LONG STORY SHORT Cut back on added salt, but use iodised salt. Choose salt-reduced products when shopping and go easy on salty foods

HUNGRY FOR MORE? See www.worldactionsonsalt.com; www.iccidd.org and search 'salt iodization'; and www.awash.org.au.

▶ Sea salt is healthier

Sea salt oozes natural food cred, and exotic and expensive coloured, single-origin salt is revered by chefs and gourmands. A quick online search reveals extraordinary claims for sea salt such as: 'one of God's gifts', 'salt-deficiency is the cause of many diseases', 'evidence for healing', and 'contains 80 mineral elements the body needs'.

The fact is, although sea salt (or any other fancy kind of salt) may add subtle differences in flavour and texture, it contains just as much harmful sodium as regular 'el cheapo' table salt. In terms of mineral content, the amounts are so small you would need to poison yourself with sodium in order to obtain useful quantities of minerals that are otherwise found in nutritious foods. For instance, one French sea salt with the highest amount of magnesium I could find only contained 0.71g per 100g. If you were to add a very generous 1 teaspoon (5g/$^1/_6$oz) of this stuff to your food on a single day, you would obtain a paltry 0.0355g (35mg) of magnesium. This is around 8–11 per cent of the Recommended Dietary Intake of magnesium for adults, but comes with a hefty 2400mg of sodium: one and a half times the 1600mg a day Suggested Dietary Target. Cheaper sea salts would offer an even worse sodium bang for your magnesium buck.

KEY FACTS All salt contains sodium. Too much sodium is harmful to your health and most of us eat way too much. The amounts of minerals in sea salt are too tiny to be of benefit.

LONG STORY SHORT If you want to stay healthy, reduce how much salt you eat from all sources—the salt you add, and the foods you buy with salt already in them.

HUNGRY FOR MORE? See www.nhlbi.nih.gov/hbp/prevent/sodium/flavor.

⊙ Gluten is harmful

The range of gluten-free food products has exploded in recent years and they are now widely available in supermarkets. This is great news for sufferers of coeliac disease and gluten intolerance, but the numbers just don't add up. Since coeliac disease affects only 1 per cent of the population, there are lots of people buying these products who don't really need to. It appears that 'gluten-free' has become the latest health fad (see *Gluten-free diets are better for you*, page 164).

The US market research company Packaged Facts conducted an online survey of almost 2000 buyers of gluten-free foods in 2010 and found the most common reason for purchase was they were 'generally healthier': 30 per cent bought them to help manage their weight and 22 per cent thought they were 'generally higher quality'. Oh dear!

Where does this idea come from that gluten-free is better and gluten is somehow bad for us? Dietitians commonly point the finger at alternative health practitioners who recommend the exclusion of wheat and gluten almost as a matter of course. Then word-of-mouth spreads the message. More products become available to meet demand, the diet becomes easier to follow, more people buy the products because they're easily available, and the trend takes hold.

It doesn't make sense that gluten is generally harmful when you consider it occurs in so many staple grain foods such as wheat, rye, barley and oats. Imagine not being able to eat regular bread, pasta, breakfast cereal, biscuits, crisp bread, cakes, thickened sauces and even enjoy a glass of beer?

Wheat and other gluten-containing grains are almost ubiquitous in western-style cuisine. Gluten adds the springy texture to bread and cakes, making gluten-free products denser and more chewy. There are also nutritional gaps in gluten-free diets, including fibre, iron and B vitamins including folate. A study published in the

British Journal of Nutrition has shown reduced numbers of friendly gut bacteria and reduced immune function in people following a gluten-free diet. The gluten-free diet isn't much fun, so why would you follow it unless you absolutely had to?

But the real issue is the gluten-free products themselves. Many are highly processed and based on high-GI ingredients such as rice and potato and some have lots of added saturated fat and sugar to enhance palatability, especially sweet biscuits, bars and cakes. Few products are based on wholegrain versions of gluten-free grains, even though wholegrains are healthier.

For those with symptoms of coeliac disease, such as abdominal pain, diarrhoea, lethargy and iron deficiency, don't self-diagnose and put yourself on a gluten-free diet. See your doctor first for a definitive diagnosis through a blood test and intestinal biopsy (following a gluten-free diet before diagnosis of coeliac disease can actually prevent a correct diagnosis being made).

If your symptoms are not due to coeliac disease, but you suspect food is somehow the cause, see a registered/accredited dietitian with experience in food intolerance to identify the real dietary culprits and create a personalised diet for you to manage your symptoms.

KEY INFO Gluten is a protein in wheat, oats, rye and barley. People with coeliac disease need a gluten-free diet for life. People with gluten intolerance feel better limiting gluten in their diet but do not need to be as strict as people with coeliac disease.

LONG STORY SHORT Only people with coeliac disease and gluten intolerance are better off eating a gluten-free diet. Some gluten-free foods aren't so healthy. If you suspect some foods may be upsetting you, have it properly investigated with a dietitian.

HUNGRY FOR MORE? See www.celiac.org (USA) or www.coeliac.org.au (Australia).

⊙ Superfoods make you super-healthy

The term 'superfood' was coined to describe foods with high levels of nutrients and phytochemicals with health benefits. Early front-runners were green leafy vegetables, berries and oily fish. However, food and supplement marketers have 'gone to town' with the whole concept and make inflated promises and exaggerated claims. I used to enjoy talking about superfoods, but now I brace myself for the next ridiculous product claim.

The first examples that come to mind are superfood supplements—not even foods at all. A cursory internet search yields wildly enthusiastic and exaggerated claims. For example, acai berries contain 'every single essential nutrient required for humans', or are 'the most perfect food on the planet'. These audacious claims are totally unsubstantiated, and if taken literally imply all you need to eat is these little berries and nothing else! And spirulina (a dried blue-green algae extract) containing '60–63%, rich vegetable protein 3–4 times higher than fish or beef'. How can this possibly be when you only take 5–10g at a time and a typical daily protein requirement is 50g? And how about the claim, '1kg of Spirulina is equivalent to 1000kg of assorted vegetables'. How silly. The obvious omission is the valuable dietary fibre component of vegetables. I wouldn't recommend giving up eating your vegetables on the basis of this ambit/crazy claim. Spirulina is also described as 'the most complete food source in the world', again suggesting a bit more than the suggested dose of 10 to 20 tablets a day may be required for this claim to be tested. And how about that dose—most people struggle to take prescribed life-saving medications or a single daily multi-vitamin, never mind 20 tablets!

Then there are the superfoods themselves. Superfruits such as acai, goji and mangosteen. They sound tantalisingly exotic, and many are unfeasibly expensive. Often they are grown in far-flung places and have to be imported dried, juiced or used as extracts for supplements. You have to question the 'natural goodness' of such processed derivatives. In Australia there is a wealth of traditional indigenous superfoods that have maintained the health of Aboriginal people for thousands of years, yet it is a growing trend to buy processed superfoods from halfway around the world. And don't get me started on the spin-off products that have spun-off most of their health benefits, such as milk chocolate-coated goji berries ($15 per 300g pack)—although I am rather fond of dark chocolate-coated incaberries as a treat because they taste divine!

Nutritional goodness does not have to cost the earth or be hard to get, as illustrated by the humble apple. Apples are one of the best and cheapest fruit sources of antioxidants around—one apple contains more antioxidants than half a punnet of blueberries or a cup of strawberries. Apples are grown within 45 minutes from my house and cost around $4 a kilogram ($2 a pound)—you do the math—and you're likely to have similar examples in your area.

Lots of foods are 'super' and work best in combination with other foods rather than on their own. It is whole diets containing a variety of different foods—not single foods or supplements— that help prevent disease and promote health and wellness. If you're into exotic superfoods and supplements and you have money to spare, then go ahead, but please regard claims with a substantial dose of scepticism. For the rest of us, health and vitality can be ours without the hefty price tag. For good health and a healthy environment, buy a variety of fresh, local, seasonal and minimally packaged produce—they're super too.

KEY INFO Superfoods have high levels of antioxidants and nutrients. When processed into a supplement, their benefits wain.
LONG STORY SHORT Superfoods and supplements are over-hyped and super-expensive. There are lots of foods that are super at less expense—aim for a variety of colours and types of fruits and

vegetables as well as wholegrains, nuts and seeds to get your quota of natural food goodness.

HUNGRY FOR MORE? Any web search using the term 'superfoods' just turns up places that want to sell you stuff you probably don't need, using claims they can't prove. And check out who paid for any 'scientific studies' that they quote.

⊙ Flaxseed oil is as good as fish oil

A client once told me she poured flaxseed oil over her breakfast cereal. My initial (private) thought was 'yuck, that can't taste good', but I was also intrigued. A web-search on flaxseed oil advertisements yielded claims bordering on the miraculous. I felt relieved she wasn't swigging it straight from the bottle! There's a lot to the omega-3 story, but here's a taste.

There are two types of omega-3 fatty acids: the long-chain marine types (EPA and DHA), and the short-chain plant type (ALA). Both the marine- and plant-type omega-3 are necessary for good health, and especially important for a healthy heart. It is recommended to consume around 2g of short-chain ALA daily to reduce heart disease risk. Flaxseed oil (also called linseed oil) is one of the richest sources of ALA. Just 1g of flaxseed oil yields around 0.6g of ALA. Some quick math shows 3–4g of flaxseed oil (less than a teaspoon) will give an optimal amount of ALA: nevertheless, pouring it on cereal is a bit over the top.

If you prefer ALA in a tastier form, a small handful of walnuts (30g) provide 3g ALA—your entire day's optimal amount, plus change. Canola oil, mustard-seed oil, soybean oil, breads and cereals containing linseed, and high-omega eggs also contain good amounts of ALA; small amounts are present in a range of other foods such as soy beans, green leafy vegetables, oats and wheatgerm. Olive oil contains very little ALA because it is monounsaturated and ALA is a polyunsaturated fat. The practical advantage of canola and soybean oils is they do not need to be kept refrigerated. Flaxseed oil will oxidise (go rancid) very quickly in the cupboard and must be kept chilled. Don't even think of cooking with flaxseed oil because it is too unstable and will degrade, releasing off-flavours and odours.

Both short-chain and long-chain omega-3 are needed, but when it comes to protection against cardiovascular disease, it is the long-chain marine-type omega-3s that have shown the most convincing benefit because of their potent anti-inflammatory and anti-arrhythmic effects (among others). The American Heart Association, British Heart Foundation and the Heart Foundation (Australia) recommend people who have already had a heart attack, or currently have angina, need 1000mg (1g) of long-chain omega-3s a day from food and/or supplements to prevent heart attack. The rest of us should consume on average 500mg daily. You can get this from two to three small serves per week of oily fish, such as swordfish, salmon, sardines, herring and tuna (check your country's recommendations on which fish to eat in order to avoid excessive mercury intake; canned tuna and salmon have very little or no mercury and do not need to be restricted). These long-chain omega-3s are not found in flaxseed oil.

In the past it was believed the body could convert short-chain ALA to the long-chain forms, and the more ALA you consumed the more EPA and DHA your body would make (thus the flaxseed on the breakfast cereal, I guess). Studies have since shown this elongation process is limited, inadequate, and varies widely between individuals. Conversion estimates vary from 0.1 to 10 per cent, and one-third of the population are unable to convert any at all. We need to get the pre-formed long-chain omega-3s as well as the short-chain ALA. So, the long and the short of it is, I'm off to shallow-fry some Atlantic salmon in canola oil, and I'll be pouring low-fat milk—not flaxseed oil—on my cereal tomorrow for breakfast. Bon appetite!

KEY INFO There are two types of omega-3: the short-chain ALA from plant foods such as flaxseed oil, canola oil and walnuts, and long-chain marine EPA and DHA from fish, seafood and eggs.
LONG STORY SHORT You need both short- and long-chain omega-3, and eating more short-chain will not convert to long-chain in adequate amounts, if at all.
HUNGRY FOR MORE? See www.omega-3centre.com.

⊙ Low-carb beer is healthier

Low-carb beer is a classic case of wishful thinking, or perhaps an example of ignoring the elephant (or the elephant beer, an extra strong beer with high alcohol content, brewed by the Carlsberg Company) in the room. Yet low-carb beers are still a hit. How could so many people have been hoodwinked into thinking a beer with less carbs is healthier **when it's the alcohol content that's the problem!** This subject inflames my passion for the whole truth on matters of food and drink.

The first rather obvious thing to point out is beer contains very low levels of carbohydrates in the first place. The average lager-style beer contains only 2 per cent carbohydrate (sugars) by volume, or 7.5g (¼oz/1½ teaspoons) in a 375ml (12fl oz) can. As a point of comparison, soft drinks contain 40g (1½oz/ 8 teaspoons) of sugar per 375ml can. You should know that carbohydrates are not especially fattening, although sugars in drinks are not a nutritious source. I like beer, and I brewed some myself as a treat with the two main men in my life: my husband and my dad. I learned the sugars added to the initial mix from malted grains are gobbled up by the brewer's yeast, which then converts them into alcohol and bubbles of carbon dioxide.

The real nail in the coffin of logic behind the marketing of low-carb beers is that they contain the same level of alcohol as regular beers, and the alcohol is the kilojoule (calorie) culprit contributing 75 per cent of the total. Alcohol contains 29kJ per gram; nearly twice that of carbohydrates (at 16kJ per gram). If you really want to curb the kilojoules, then drinking low-alcohol, or 'light' beer makes much more sense. Of course, you wouldn't know this because alcoholic beverages don't require nutrition labelling—which is stupid when foods have to. Most people have no clue how many calories they put away when they sink a few.

So what's really going on behind the low-carb beer phenomenon? I'm sure you'll have your own ideas, but I go back to my original assertion that it's all just wishful thinking. As hedonistic souls prone to excess (especially during holidays), perhaps low-carb beers give us permission to drink more? Maybe men consider low-alcohol beer an affront to their masculinity but low-carb is OK because their personal trainer drinks it? I think it's more that savvy marketers are good at finding the soft underbelly of human nature and cashing in on it. And of course it is a bit funny to see folks chowing down on burgers, fries and other fatty fare with a low-carb beer on the side!

KEY INFO Beer is not high in carbs: the alcohol provides the majority of calories. Low-alcohol beer is the best choice for health-conscious beer drinker.

LONG STORY SHORT It's blindingly obvious really, but if you're interested in a 'six-pack' stomach rather than a beer-barrel body, drink less beer.

HUNGRY FOR MORE? See www.calorieking.com and check out the calorie content of drinks, and www.nhmrc.gov.au/publications/synopses/ds10syn and www.cdc.gov/alcohol/fact-sheets/alcohol-use and www.drinkaware.co.uk on how to reduce health risks from alcohol.

▶ You get all the Vitamin D you need from the sun

This has always been one of my faves ...

My mother was recently told she had low vitamin D levels. I was quite surprised as she is an active woman who loves the outdoors and spending time in her garden. Living in a sunny country like Australia, surely she gets enough 'sunshine vitamin'? Looking into this subject further, I discovered low vitamin D levels are a real problem for many people, especially older people whose skin is less efficient at making vitamin D from sunshine. People over 70 need three times as much vitamin D as those under 50.

The risk of vitamin D deficiency also increases if you live in less sunny climates, if you have dark skin, don't expose your skin to the sun and always cover up and wear high-protection sunscreen. My mother's low vitamin D levels now start to make sense—she has taken skin cancer prevention very much on board and never goes outside without sunscreen, a long-sleeved shirt and a hat. We have all been bombarded with the 'slip, slop, slap' skin protection message for decades in an effort to bring down the high incidence of melanoma skin cancer. Low vitamin D levels are also passed on from mother to baby as vitamin D-deficient mothers make vitamin D-deficient breast-milk. Obese people are more likely to have low vitamin D because it is fat-soluble and gets trapped in body fat unable to travel around the body to where it is needed.

What does vitamin D do? It is vital for utilising calcium and maintaining strong bones. In fact my mother's vitamin D status was discovered when she broke a rib after falling off a ladder—ouch! But the magic of vitamin D doesn't end with bones. It is implicated in protection against cancer, Parkinson's disease and high blood pressure; regulating the immune system; and insulin secretion and blood glucose control. Research has also found a strong correlation between having higher vitamin D levels and higher HDL (good) cholesterol levels. A recent study also found a link between low vitamin D levels and depression suggesting vitamin D can boost mood—giving new support for the idea of a 'sunny disposition'.

Vitamin D deficiency requires supplementation to correct, but how can it be prevented? It makes sense to get some sunshine each day if possible. Dietary sources also have taken on renewed importance. Foods containing vitamin D include some fatty fish (mackerel, salmon, sardines) and fish liver oils, as well as small amounts in liver, cheese and eggs. In the US, milk is fortified with vitamin D but in other countries vitamin D is added only to some brands of dairy foods and milk alternatives (eg, soy milk). Margarine spreads usually have vitamin D added, making them good to include for general good health as well as healthier cholesterol levels (see *Butter is better than margarine because it's natural*, page 101).

KEY INFO Vitamin D is a 'rock star vitamin' with many important functions. Even in sunny places, a significant number of people can be low in vitamin D.

LONG STORY SHORT It is important to get a little sun each day if possible (but not enough to burn the skin) as well as to eat foods with vitamin D. In Australia, extra care is needed with safe sun exposure because the sun's UV rays are more intense (see link below).

HUNGRY FOR MORE? See http://ods.od.nih.gov/factsheets/vitamind and www.cancer.org.au/File/Cancersmartlifestyle/Howmuchsunisenough.

⊙ Raw foods are best

I love vegetables! All kinds, including the uncooked ones. Nothing beats the crunch of a raw carrot, or the crispness of lettuce and cucumber in a salad. However, you can take a good idea to extremes. There is a whole diet tribe who only eat raw foods, believing it to be best for health, wellbeing, longevity and prevention of disease. It's kind of like the advanced, super-duper version of the vegan diet (no animal foods). Raw-food diet followers exist on raw vegetables, fruits, nuts, seeds, sprouted beans and seaweed—none of which can be heated above 37.8°C (116°F), about body temperature—or else they believe enzymes will be destroyed and the food won't be as well digested and absorbed. This is a load of rubbish. The enzymes are for the plants' benefit, not ours! Human beings have huge brains and smaller jaws and a smaller digestive tract than our primitive ancestors because we discoverd fire and learned how to cook food. The raw food diet is best suited to the early hominids such as Australopithecus afarensis that roamed the Earth several million years ago.

The nutritional shortfalls of not eating any animal foods, such as meat, fish, milk and eggs, are obvious (see *Vegetarian diets are healthier,* page 32), but the idea that plant foods should be eaten raw to extract their nutrition is just false. In fact, so called 'anti-nutrient' factors in raw plant foods make them harder to digest. Phytates can reduce absorption of minerals such as iron and zinc, and nuts contain enzyme inhibitors in the skin. Of course, the level of some vitamins (such as vitamin C) and antioxidants (sulforaphane) are reduced by the cooking process; however, in a mixed diet this is not an issue (still, don't boil the life out of your vegetables but lightly steam, microwave, stir-fry or roast them instead).

Processing vegetables by juicing, mashing, pureeing or cooking actually releases more vitamins and antioxidants from vegetables than eating them raw and whole. For example, more lycopene (an antioxidant) is absorbed from a tomato pasta sauce than raw tomatoes, and the same goes for beta-carotene from carrots. The physical effects, as well as higher temperature, soften and break the tough cell walls in plant foods so their inner goodies can be released. In fact, an Italian study comparing steaming, boiling and frying found all methods increased the availability of antioxidants in zucchini (courgettes), carrots and broccoli. The availability of cancer-fighting indoles in cruciferous vegetables such as cabbage is also higher after cooking.

If it's weight loss you want, the raw-food diet is very effective. This is because most foods you can easily get hold of are off-limits. Burger? Nope. Cake? No, again. Pancakes? Nah. Sunday roast? Definitely not. Weight loss is also assured because of the hard work in chewing and digesting raw foods, as well as how much longer they take to prepare and eat. Raw foodists say they feel fabulous and have loads of energy and vitality, but I think much of this is due to 'dieters' high' (the feeling of wellbeing you get when losing weight) or simply because they have banished all the crap food they used to eat.

Because it is very bulky, high in fibre and nutrient-sparse, a raw food diet carries a very high risk for people with higher nutritional needs, such as children and pregnant women—they need a lot of nutrients the body can easily get at. If you have sensitive bowels, such as Irritable Bowel Syndrome, this diet will only lead to tears (from pain in your gut) because of its very high fibre content. And the taste? I'll leave that for you to decide, but I contend this is an extreme diet you do out of conviction rather than enjoyment.

I would recommend anyone trying the raw food diet to take a supplement designed for vegans, and also give up your day job— you'll need the time to shop for and prepare your food. In the raw food world, it's the committed or the hungry.

KEY INFO Raw foods contain substances that can reduce the availability of nutrients. Cooking does reduce some vitamins, but some nutrients and phytochemicals become more available to the body after cooking. There are nutritional pros and cons of both raw and cooked food.

LONG STORY SHORT Besides being a heck of a lot of trouble, you do not need to follow a raw-food diet to be healthy. Enjoy a balanced diet from all the food groups and a variety of raw and cooked foods.

HUNGRY FOR MORE? Read Richard Wrangham's book, *Catching Fire: How Cooking Made Us Human*.

⊙ Vitamin C cures colds

Vitamin C has received a lot of attention as an immune booster, particularly against colds. But before you reach for vitamin C tablets at the first sign of a sniffle, taking vitamin C when you already have a cold probably won't help, and nor will taking it to prevent colds. Ensuring you get at least 200mg of vitamin C daily over the long term may strengthen your defences and reduce the duration and severity of colds when they occur. This amount of vitamin C is achievable in a healthy diet with the recommended two fruits and five serves of vegetables daily. Vitamin C supplements can vary but may contain up to 2000mg of vitamin C (ten times more than you need!). Because it is water soluble, any excess is passed out in the urine, but large doses can irritate your digestive tract.

Supplementation under extreme cold and stress conditions (eg, working in the Arctic) or extreme physical exertion (eg, marathon running) might help, but under normal circumstances taking vitamin C tablets does not prevent colds. A review of studies found a small and probably unnoticeable reduction in the duration of colds in people taking more than 200mg of vitamin C a day as tablets.

Boosting antioxidant-rich fruit and vegetables is the best defence against winter sniffles and sneezes. Vitamin C-rich foods include fruits (citrus, berries, guava, mangoes, pineapple) and vegetables (cabbage, cauliflower, capsicum/pepper). Vitamin C is pretty easy to come by if you eat your fruit and veggies, even if you don't like oranges.

In the fight against colds and flu, it is vitamin D rather than vitamin C that is attracting all the headlines. Studies indicate people with higher levels of vitamin D have a lower risk of respiratory infections (see *You get all the Vitamin D you need from the sun*, page 200).

KEY INFO Vitamin C is important for a healthy immune system; however, mega-doses are not needed and supplements are not the best way to get it. Vitamin D is also important for immune defence against colds and flu.

LONG STORY SHORT To prevent colds and flu you need to eat enough vitamin C-rich foods all the time. Taking vitamin C supplements will not help much once you have a cold. Eating a wide range of fruit and vegetables each day will give you the best mix of antioxidants, and in the right amounts.

HUNGRY FOR MORE? See www.health.harvard.edu/flu-resource-center/how-to-boost-your-immune-system.

⊙ The Mediterranean diet is healthy because of the olive oil

Everybody has heard good things about the Mediterranean diet. Typically, we hear it's good for the heart, because of the lower rates of heart disease in countries surrounding the Mediterranean Sea. However, when asked what's healthy about it, most people almost always say olive oil. This is not the whole story.

The traditional Mediterranean diet—predominantly plant-food based—contains a bounty of foods with known protective effects: vegetables, fruits, grains, legumes, nuts, herbs and spices; fish; and small servings of alcohol and red meat. The mechanism of protection is still not fully understood, but there are likely to be many different protective effects offered by different foods (and the alcohol). The olive oil may just help the plant foods taste great enough so you eat loads of them (anyone who has eaten in a traditional Greek home will know it's vegetables a-go-go). And there are non-diet factors too. For many traditional communities around the Mediterranean, their lives are simpler, they are more physically active and religion is central to everyday life. You could say religion is crucial to the health benefits of Mediterranean diet!

Why is the question 'what's healthy about the Mediterranean diet?' important? Well, so we can steal the good parts for our own diet—like leafy greens and legumes. But I've met people who just don't like the taste of olive oil (we must not judge …).

Although olive oil is a healthy choice, it may have a neutral effect on heart health by displacing bad fats rather than actively protecting by itself. Olive oil is primarily monounsaturated and there is little evidence that monounsaturated fats in olive oil have a direct effect on reducing the risk of heart disease so don't rely on them alone to prevent a heart attack. Another component of olive oil often mentioned is the antioxidants (polyphenolic compounds), particularly high in extra virgin olive oil. These are likely to be beneficial, but they are not unique to olive oil. Thousands of phytochemicals exist across all plant foods.

An even better result may be achieved with a modified Mediterranean diet that uses sunflower or canola oil instead of olive oil. This is because polyunsaturated fats have greater cholesterol-lowering effects, and because of the known benefits of omega-6 and omega-3 fats. This idea of a Mediterranean-style diet using a different oil—in this instance, canola oil and margarine—yielded spectacular results in the famous Lyon Heart Study. This seminal study showed an impressive 76 per cent reduction in risk of death or major coronary events (eg, heart attack, stroke etc) in patients who had previously had a heart attack (and thus were at high risk) after following a modified Mediterranean diet for 27 months.

If you want to eat a healthy diet, then try to take all the leaves out of the Mediterranean diet book rather than just the page on olive oil, or you're bound to come up short on benefits (which reminds me, don't forget to eat lots of leafy greens). A heart-healthy diet is a whole rather than one or two parts, and can be adapted to suit individual and cultural preferences.

KEY INFO Olive oil is monounsaturated and less protective than polyunsaturated oils such as sunflower and canola. A modified Mediterranean diet with canola oil is also highly protective against heart disease. The Mediterranean diet is healthy because it is predominantly plant-food based. The people who traditionally followed it had healthy active lifestyles, spiritual conviction and strong social connections.

LONG STORY SHORT To protect your heart, eat a mostly plant-based diet, including wholegrains, vegetables, legumes, fruits, nuts and seeds. Enjoy a variety of oils, including polyunsaturated types such as sunflower and canola oil, as well as some monounsaturated types such as olive oil if you like it. Keep meat portions small and lean and include fish twice a week. If you drink alcohol, stop at one or two standard drinks a day.

Hungry for more? See www.oldwayspt.org/mediterraneandiet.

The Lyon Diet Heart Study

This was a randomised control trial of subjects known to have had a previous heart attack. The goal was to test the effectiveness of a modified Mediterranean-style diet on preventing recurrent heart attacks compared with a western-type diet over a five-year period. Patients under the age of 70 years old who were hospitalised for a heart attack were asked to participate in the study. Those who agreed were randomised into two diet groups. The experimental group, with 302 subjects, was asked to follow a modified Mediterranean-style diet. The control group, with 303 subjects, was not provided dietary instructions, but was asked by their doctors to follow a 'prudent' diet.

The subjects in the experimental group were asked to consume a diet high in fruits and vegetables, particularly root and green vegetables, olive oil, bread, legumes, and eat more fish and poultry and less red meat, lamb and pork. Butter and cream was replaced with a canola oil-based margarine containing alpha-linolenic acid (short-chain omega-3).

The original study was stopped because the modified Mediterranean diet was so effective in reducing the risk of heart attack that the researchers felt they could not withhold such a significant benefit from the control group.

⊙ Eggs increase cholesterol

Ever wondered why egg-white omelettes became so popular? Heaven knows, it wasn't for the flavour! It's a classic case of food egg-stremism resulting in the poor old egg copping a bad rap. Eggs were shunned because of their cholesterol content. But looking a little deeper we find eating eggs is not linked with higher rates of heart disease. Although eggs contain cholesterol, eating eggs in moderation as part of a heart-friendly diet low in saturated fat will not adversely affect the blood cholesterol level of most people.

Blood cholesterol levels are far more influenced by how much saturated and trans-fat you eat than dietary cholesterol. A typical 50g egg contains 5g fat, of which only 1.5g is saturated. Eggs are full of vitamins and minerals, such as vitamin A, E, folate and B12, antioxidants lutein and zeaxanthin, which help maintain healthy eyes, and also contain long-chain omega-3 fats (like the ones in fish).

However, like most foods it appears you can have too much of a good thing. More than one egg a day is excessive any way you look at it. Yet again, the old nutrition wisdom prevails—enjoy everything in moderation.

KEY INFO What's moderation? Most of us can enjoy up to six eggs a week as part of a healthy balanced (and heart-friendly) diet. Australians eat an average of three eggs a week, so there's no need to worry. Egg-streme egg eating may only increase cholesterol in the super-sensitive (who are probably on medication for cholesterol anyway). Some research suggests people with diabetes should stop at three to four eggs a week, but I think it's a storm in an egg-cup.

LONG STORY SHORT The common belief that eggs cause high cholesterol is wrong. Cholesterol in food like eggs and shellfish doesn't add to blood cholesterol levels. Enjoy eggs together with protective plant foods such as wholegrains, vegetables, legumes, fish, nuts and healthy oils. Think ... egg, beans and mushrooms on mixed grain muffins, or, avocado and scrambled eggs rather than a greasy fry-up with bacon, white toast, butter and salt.

HUNGRY FOR MORE? See www.enc-online.org, content approved by scientific advisory panel convened by the egg industry and www. heartfoundation.org.au/healthy-eating/food-and-nutrition-facts/Pages/egg-legumes-pulses-nuts-seeds.

⊙ Acidic foods are bad for arthritis

Some 50 million Americans and four million Australians have some form of arthritis. More than 10 million adults in the UK consult their GP each year with arthritis and related conditions. Osteoarthritis, rheumatoid arthritis and gout account for 95 per cent of all cases. It's a major cause of disability and chronic pain, which is probably why there are so many myths about food and arthritis because, being human, we want to feel we can DO something to feel better. And looking at what we eat seems a good place to start in the search for a magic bullet!

According to Arthritis Research UK, there is no reason to avoid acid foods such as oranges, mandarins, lemons, limes and tomatoes causes arthritis. And cutting them out of your diet means that you are cutting out fruits that are great sources of vitamin C and antioxidants and help lower the overall GI of your diet. And in the case of tomatoes, you'd be cutting out a rich source of lycopene, which is associated with a reduced risk of prostate cancer—a good thing for men.

'Acid' seems to be the word that worries people. Look at it like this: where your body is concerned, few foods are as acid as your very own digestive juices. Once in the stomach, all foods are acidic!

Gout is another matter. Some foods DO appear to trigger gout attacks in some people. These are foods that have high levels of purine, a substance we turn into uric acid in our bodies. Interestingly, the problem foods aren't ones you'd put at the top of your 'acidic food' list. Instead they are fishy foods such as sardines, anchovies, mackerel and herrings; offal meats like kidneys and liver; shellfish and yeast.

KEY INFO There's no proof at all that acidic foods, or dairy foods, or foods from the nightshade family—potatoes, eggplant and capsicum (tomatoes belong here too)—cause arthritis.

Long story short No diet we know of can cure arthritis. A healthy balanced diet is best. And you have to get moving. Pain relief comes with exercise because physical activity strengthens and supports the joints. Losing a bit of weight helps too.

Hungry for more? See www.arthritisresearchuk.org and search for 'diet' and www.cdc.gov/arthritis. Arthritis Australia has a great website and information sheets you can download; go to www.arthritisaustralia.com.au.

⊙ Kids don't get high cholesterol

Age is no barrier. Children can have high cholesterol—the numbers are increasing in step with the number of children who are overweight and obese. The risk factors are the same as those for adults: being overweight or obese, eating too much saturated fat and having a family history of high cholesterol.

So why is this important? Unfortunately, the longer the body carries too much cholesterol around in the blood, the greater the chances of a heart attack or stroke. Children who have high cholesterol are more likely to experience these devastating events at an earlier adult age when they are in the prime of their lives in their thirties and forties with children and financial commitments.

Because children learn what and how to eat from their parents, healthy eating starts with those first foods. High blood cholesterol in kids and adults can be prevented or reduced by enjoying a combination of heart-friendly foods and getting moving. The evidence is convincing that diet works without side effects and nourishes the whole family as well.

Even if your family is low risk, switching to reduced-fat milk when children are two years is recommended. This will help everyone's cholesterol to stay down, and prevents 'multi-milk confusion' in your refrigerator. As many household nutrition managers and grocery buyers (mums and dads) will attest, the family will eat/drink what's there.

KEY INFO We are now seeing signs of heart disease (fatty streaks in the arteries) in children, especially if they are overweight. And the rates of children with type 2 diabetes is increasing; twenty years ago it was virtually unheard of in this age group.
LONG STORY SHORT Children need to 'eat to beat cholesterol' as much as grown-ups to keep their hearts healthy. It's a family affair and the solution lies with the food on our plates and the miles on our dials.

How the whole family can eat to beat cholesterol

- Eat at least five serves of vegetables daily from a variety of colours and types. Enjoy them with a little healthy oil for taste and to better absorb their antioxidants.
- Enjoy at least two serves of fruit daily—one serve is the size of an average apple.
- Boost natural food flavours with herbs and spices to eat less sodium (salt).
- Ensure half your grain foods are wholegrains (at least two serves daily—eg, two slices of wholemeal bread and a bowl of wholegrain cereal).
- Include low-GI foods at most meals—multigrain bread, pasta, barley, sweetcorn, high-fibre breakfast cereals, muesli, porridge, most fruits, legumes, and low-fat milk and yoghurt. Check the GI of foods at www.glycemicindex.com.
- Include legumes such as beans, chickpeas or lentils in at least two meals per week (more is better).
- Enjoy 30g (one small handful) of nuts most days. They're highly nutritious and packed full of heart-friendly nutrients.
- Enjoy fish at least twice a week (preferably oily fish) for protective omega-3 fats.
- Enjoy at least one-and-a-half tablespoons of healthy oils and spreads daily as these 'tip the balance' toward unsaturated fats, which lower cholesterol. Healthy oils include canola, olive, mustard seed, macadamia nut, peanut, rice bran, safflower, sesame, sunflower, soybean and walnut oils, and trans-fat free margarine.

HUNGRY FOR MORE? See *Saturated fats aren't that bad*, page 184; *The butter vs marg debate*, pages 100–05; *Eggs increase cholesterol*, page 210; and *Shellfish and offal are bad for cholesterol*, page 216.

⊙ Shellfish and offal are bad for cholesterol

The dietary cholesterol in shellfish (prawns, scallops, oysters) and offal meats (liver, kidneys, brains, tongue) doesn't make a significant contribution to your blood cholesterol levels. The high blood cholesterol culprits in your diet are more likely to be the saturated and trans-fats you are eating.

Shellfish bring a bounty of nutritional goodness—they are rich in protein, contain heart-friendly omega-3 fats and, when harvested from the sea, are a good source of dietary iodine, an essential trace element important for thyroid function and metabolism. They are low in total and saturated fat. Besides, most people don't consume shellfish often or in large amounts.

As for offal (what the Americans call 'variety meats' and in Italy is known as quinto quarto – the fifth quarter), we tend to turn our nose up about eating it these days, which is a pity as it packs a punch when it comes to nutritional goodies. Liver, for example, is rich in iron, a mineral many people are short on and isn't 'fatty': a 100g (3½oz) serving of grilled calf's liver contains 8g (less than ¹/₃oz) fat, of which just under 3g is saturated. Eating offal is not just good for you, it's good for the planet as you are eating parts of the beast that might otherwise be wasted. It's called 'nose-to-tail' eating.

KEY INFO You can include some cholesterol-rich foods, such as offal (calf's liver, lamb's fry and kidneys) and shellfish as part of a healthy balanced diet low in saturated and trans-fats.

LONG STORY SHORT It's how you cook it that counts. Moderate serves of offal meats and shellfish are good for you unless coated in batter and deep fried or crumbed and tossed in a pan of butter.

HUNGRY FOR MORE? See also *Eggs increase cholesterol*, page 210.

⊙ Sports drinks are better than water

Around two-thirds of the body is water, and every process depends upon it. We lose it simply by breathing, sweating and urinating, so we need to replace it. That's why it's a good habit to drink plenty of water each day, but we need more to prevent dehydration if we exercise, especially in the heat. This is because the body uses fluids to keep cool, and getting too hot can compromise performance.

Cool drinks absorb faster and, for most of us, water is the best choice. Drink 250–500ml (1–2 cups) before exercise, 125ml (½ cup) for every 15 minutes of exercise and 500ml at the end to replace lost fluids. A good way to see if you've replaced lost fluids is to check the colour of your urine—the darker the colour, the more you need to drink. When you're well hydrated your urine should be almost clear (except for the first wee after you wake in the morning).

Don't get dehydrated

Severe dehydration is life-threatening, but even mild dehydration can cause headaches, muscle ache and fatigue. Over the long term, inadequate fluid intake can increase the risk of kidney stones and cancers of the bowel and urinary tract. Drinking enough fluids helps boost mental and physical performance and can reduce overeating, as it helps us feel full.

Sports drinks were designed for elite athletes but may benefit the rest of us during long periods of serious exercise (more than an hour). Available in a range of flavours, they contain salts (electrolytes) and carbohydrate in the right proportions for rehydration and endurance. Sports and flavoured-water products with less sugar are also available. The addition of vitamins and herbs may make them more appealing, but it's little more than window dressing. A balanced and varied diet will provide all you need of these.

Sports drinks are an effective and convenient tonic for dehydration, especially after a night on the booze or a bout of gastro', although oral rehydration products you can buy at the pharmacy are better (especially for children).

KEY INFO Keep cool by drinking plenty of fluids before, during and after exercise.

LONG STORY SHORT For most of us most of the time, water is best. Sports drinks offer real advantages for serious athletes and those exercising longer than an hour.

HUNGRY FOR MORE? See also *Everyone should drink eight glasses of water a day*, page 182; *Tea and coffee are dehydrating*, page 170.

⊙ Eat some dark chocolate every day for the antioxidants

'It has antioxidants' is the latest in a long line of excuses chocolate lovers have come up with to justify their desires. This one has some science on its side.

Cocoa beans are naturally rich in flavonoid antioxidants. Four to six small squares (25g/1oz) of dark chocolate provides about the same amount of these antioxidants as half a cup of black tea or a glass of red wine. Milk chocolate has only one-third the antioxidants of dark chocolate and white chocolate has none at all.

Beware treat creep

Treats are one of the nice things in life. Not everyone needs treat foods every day, but it's better to allow yourself some treat foods so you don't create cravings that lead to binges.

Keep the portions small and track them over the day as treat creep is all too easy and 'occasional reward' has suddenly turned into 'constant reward'. For most of us, one small treat a day is OK, but 'less is best' if you want to lose weight.

What's a treat? Think of it as being equivalent to 600kJ. That's:

- 4– 6 small squares (½ small bar) dark chocolate (25g/¾oz)
- 2 scoops low-fat vanilla ice cream
- 4 small plain or 2 rich (eg, chocolate or cream) biscuits
- 1 small packet (30g/1oz) potato crisps.

And remember that treats don't have to be food. Reward yourself with something you like to do—taking time out for a walk in the sunshine, a swim or a surf; walking the dog; calling a friend, downloading music; buying some flowers; having your hair done or relaxing with a foot massage.

It's believed that the antioxidants in dark chocolate may help prevent cholesterol from sticking to the walls of blood vessels, relax major blood vessels (help them be less stiff and more flexible), decrease blood pressure, and maybe even prevent blood from becoming 'sticky' and forming clots.

The downside is that dark chocolate (like all other chocolate) is energy-dense—you get a lot of kilojoules in a small amount—and is high in saturated fat, which is why it's a treat food.

You don't need to tuck into dark chocolate every day for these beneficial antioxidants because other foods and beverages—such as green and black tea, red wine, certain fruits (berries, black grapes, plums, apples) and vegetables (artichokes, asparagus, cabbage, russet and sweet potatoes)—are good sources of them too.

KEY INFO A good rule of thumb is that 'dark and rich' is best. In terms of antioxidant content, dark chocolate is top of the benefit tree. High cocoa chocolate contains up to 70 per cent cocoa and the percentage is usually on the label.

LONG STORY SHORT Dark chocolate can fit into a healthy eating plan, but moderation is the key. Savour SMALL portions as a treat that brings some beneficial antioxidants—and just for the taste and enjoyment of it.

HUNGRY FOR MORE? See www.cacaoweb.net/nutrition and www. heartfoundation.org.au and search 'antioxidants'.

⊙ Green tea is better for you

All regular tea is made from the leaves of *Camellia sinensis*, which are picked and dried to make green or black tea. Green tea is lightly steamed soon after picking to suspend oxidative changes. Black tea is allowed to oxidise and oolong tea is partially oxidised. Both black and green teas contain flavonoid antioxidants—just different types.

Green tea contains more simple flavonoids called catechins; black tea has more complex ones called theaflavins and thearubigins thanks to the oxidising process.

Regular tea drinkers (three to four cups a day) have a reduced risk of heart disease and stroke, according to population studies. Although it's not yet clear exactly how tea does this, the protection seems to be the flavonoid content.

Green tea tends to hit the headlines because of studies suggesting that its catechins may help with weight loss. The catechins in green tea are unique and have very long names that are usually shortened, the best known being EGCG. Green tea experiments have shown it increases the amount of energy burned and the use of fat as fuel in the body, leading to better weight and body fat loss. It all sound promising, but it's no magic bullet and much more research is needed.

Canned or bottled 'iced teas' aren't a substitute for hot tea. They have quite a bit of sugar added (although less than soft drink)—think of them as a 'slightly better for you' soft drink alternative.

Key info If you want to do something really good for yourself, drink tea—green, oolong or black. And don't rush it, because the longer you leave it to brew the higher the flavonoid antioxidant content. For the best flavour, allow regular black tea to brew for three minutes, green tea for four minutes and oolong tea for six minutes. Adding milk (low-fat, of course) doesn't affect the antioxidant activity.

LONG STORY SHORT Tea drinking isn't a good, better, best story. It's all good in moderation (that's those three to four cups a day), so take time and make yourself a cuppa with tea leaves or teabags, whichever you prefer.

HUNGRY FOR MORE? See *Tea and coffee are dehydrating*, page 170.

What about herb teas?

Herb teas aren't technically teas: they are 'infusions' made from herbs, spices and/or flowers, not *C. sinensis*. They don't contain the flavonoid antioxidants that regular tea does (although they contain others which are less studied), but they can make a tasty contribution to your daily fluids for hydration.

⊙ Spinach is a good source of iron

This is a yes and a no. Thanks to Popeye, we tuck into spinach (raw or cooked), thinking it's a good source of iron. It is, but that iron doesn't get into our body in great amounts (we say it isn't well absorbed).

When it comes to iron, you need to know that there are two types and there is a difference.

- Haem iron is found in animal foods, such as meat, chicken, fish and offal.
- Non-haem iron is found in eggs, legumes, cereal grains, nuts, seeds, dark green leafy vegetables (eg, spinach and broccoli) and dried fruit.

The difference matters because our bodies can absorb haem iron much more readily than non-haem iron. In fact, the body absorbs around 15–25 per cent of haem iron from animal sources, but only around 2–5 per cent of non-haem iron from plant sources like spinach.

The good news is you can greatly increase absorption of non-haem iron if you consume fruit and veggies rich in vitamin C at the same time, such as having sliced fruit on your breakfast cereal or salad with your wholegrain sandwich—it helps your body absorb the iron in the cereal and bread.

The bad news: some natural compounds found in plants such as phytates and oxalates (in spinach, rhubarb, chard and beet greens) as well as tannins in tea and coffee can inhibit the absorption of iron. This is because they bind and hold iron so that your body can't absorb it properly. However, eating a wide variety of foods over the day should ensure that the benefits of vitamin C intake override the phytate effect. And the news isn't all bad for phytates: in fact they are an antioxidant with anti-inflammatory and anti-cancer effects and help to lower the glycemic index (GI) of foods.

KEY INFO Spinach is packed with vitamins—it's an excellent source of vitamin C, folate, beta carotene (which is converted into vitamin A in the body) along with some vitamin E and gives us important antioxidants such as lutein and zeaxanthin, which help to keep the eye disease macular degeneration at bay as we grow older. It is not, however, a good source of easily absorbed iron.

LONG STORY SHORT The best sources of iron are lean red meat, chicken and fish. Vegetables are a useful way to top up your daily iron intake (and much more besides) and best sources are the dark green leafy vegetables including spinach, broccoli, Asian greens, collard and kale.

HUNGRY FOR MORE? See www.cdc.gov/nutrition/everyone/basics/vitamins/iron.

PART 4

Food in modern living

Let's face it; we live in a very different world to that of our forebears. We work hard and don't have a lot of time to source and prepare our food, and expect others to do much of the work for us. Food technology has advanced in leaps and bounds. While many pour scorn on the food industry, those of us living in wealthy countries are spoiled for choice of what to eat. Sure, we need to be selective to look after our health but there are lots of myths that—if true—just make life harder. Healthy eating in the modern age need not be an extreme sport. Read on and take comfort that a bit of common sense is an important tool to navigate the modern food jungle.

⊙ Processed foods are bad

I get a bit annoyed at holier-than-thou health nuts who say we should avoid all 'processed' foods. It sounds great—indeed virtuous—but in reality it's both impractical and undesirable for regular folk who are busy trying to keep work, home and family together. The term 'processed' is nutritionally meaningless without further qualifiers, like 'highly' 'or 'over'. Just about all foods are processed in one way or another; just think of basics like low-fat milk, bread, porridge oats and muesli. There's a reason why food processing and technology have made leaps and bounds—because we, the consumers, have demanded it. I'm not saying all technological advances are used to promote health, but on balance it's been a great leap forward for society. Processed food is the price we pay for the life we desire, and we can't go back. To support a global population of nine billion—mostly urbanised—by 2050 we're going to need more technology to help feed the world, not less.

We now spend less time on shopping and preparing food. We demanded this because women moved out of the kitchen and into the workforce. Unfortunately, men haven't assumed their share of the domestic tasks—including cooking—and the food industry has picked up the slack. It now takes 30 minutes rather than three hours to whip up spaghetti bolognese using dried pasta, frozen mince, a bottled sauce and some bagged salad; an incredible feat of modern food technology when you think about it. The same meal could take several hours to prepare from scratch (plus the toil of preserving the previous summer's tomato crop). Although many people moan about supermarkets, they give us most things we want (and lots we shouldn't want) all under the one roof: easy.

Processing food allows us to enjoy food from around the world. Could you imagine only being able to eat fresh food from your local area? And then having to preserve what you couldn't consume in a few days? Buying local where you can is a great thing, but the 100-mile diet (and others like it) is unrealistic for most people.

The UK, USA, Canada, Australia and New Zealand are cultural melting pots and processed foods allow migrants to enjoy the tastes of home and the rest of us to expand our culinary horizons. International trade in food supports many developing countries as well as developed ones.

Food technology and food additives reduce food waste by prolonging shelf life and preserving seasonal produce. Although there are some unfortunate individuals who are sensitive to certain food additives (labelling makes avoidance easy), their benefits are still worth it for society at large. We forget about the untold millions of lives saved due to preservatives stopping the growth of deadly bacteria. The huge consumer concern about food additives is disproportionate to the actual evidence of harm. They undergo safety testing before they are permitted in foods and there has never been a single reported death attributed to a food additive. Eating too much salt is responsible for millions of deaths globally but it doesn't attract the same antipathy as additives because it doesn't need a code number. We have very high standards for the food we buy but fail to recognise the role of additives in producing its desired safety, colour, texture and flavour.

I applaud taking more time to buy quality fresh local produce and preparing it at home with love and care because this brings a range of health, environmental and social benefits. But I'd rather be choosing from the wonderful diversity of fresh and healthier 'processed' foods than wearing an apron 24/7. I think I'll treat myself tonight with some low-fat (and low-GI) vanilla ice cream, raspberries (from the freezer) and dark chocolate shavings, followed by a decaf coffee. Try making those from scratch ...

KEY INFO Food technology has followed massive social change and allows us to eat safe, varied and convenient foods. Although many people believe food additives are harmful, they are safe (although a small number of people may be sensitive to them).

LONG STORY SHORT Fresh food is great but our lifestyles no longer permit eating only fresh food. 'Processed' food can make a significant contribution to health, convenience and enjoyment HUNGRY FOR MORE? See *Food additives are harmful*, page 231; and www.foodinsight.org.

Processed foods to the rescue

The take-home message of 2011 with the catastrophic earthquakes and aftershocks in New Zealand and Japan, the big freeze in Europe, blizzards and tornadoes in the US and disastrous floods in Australia, Brazil and Sri Lanka, is that preparing for an emergency is the smart thing to do. Bush fires, cyclones, tornadoes, tsunamis, floods, earthquakes and blizzards could leave you trapped without electricity or gas. It's vital to have SAFE ready-to-eat food on hand to keep you and your family fighting fit. And this is where processed foods shine. Opt for low(er) salt/sodium products when there is a choice and check use-by dates. Drain canned foods and rinse if you have clean water. Here's my ten top processed pantry picks for an emergency.

1. Canned beans, chickpeas and lentils
2. Canned fish
3. Canned meats and meat dishes
4. Cans and jars of fruit in natural juice
5. Cans and jars of vegetables
6. Nuts (not salted), seeds and mixes
7. Dry cereals, such as fruit and nut muesli, muesli bars
8. Grainy crackers and shelf-stable flat breads
9. Powdered milk and small containers of UHT milks (dairy, almond, oat or soy)
10. Bottled water and diet soft drinks

⊙ Food additives are harmful

Food additives must be proven safe before they are allowed to be added to foods. Food additives are regulated country to country, but countries also take advice from an international body called Codex Alimentarius, (or 'Codex' for short), which is part of the World Health Organisation. In the UK and Europe, food additives are regulated by the European Union, in the USA by the Food & Drug Administration (FDA), and in Australia and New Zealand, by Food Standards Australia and New Zealand (FSANZ). A key purpose of these regulations and Codex is to protect public health by ensuring food is safe to eat.

Food and additives manufacturers must jump through many hoops before they can use a new additive. A new additive must go through a rigorous safety assessment. Part of the safety assessment involves estimating how much of the additive is likely to be eaten compared with the recognised Acceptable Daily Intake (ADI). The ADI is the amount of an additive that could be eaten every day over an entire lifetime without harm. Regulators also keep tabs on the scientific evidence regarding already approved additives. If new information emerges about possible harm, it is assessed and additives can be withdrawn from use if necessary. Additives are only approved to be used in certain foods to prevent us eating too much of any one additive.

So why do food additives have such a bad reputation? Some folks just can't believe any food technology can be beneficial: they're the ones suggesting we go back to growing our food and cooking all fresh food from scratch. They overly romanticise the past and forget that food technology has allowed us to eat better, live longer and double the world population. There are misunderstandings about 'chemicals' in our food when in fact all foods (and indeed ourselves) are made up of chemicals: just because you can't pronounce something doesn't mean it is bad. There are also a few loud conspiracy theorists who think the food

Examples of additives from nature

Additive Number	Additive Name	Additive Function	What is it?
100	curcumin or turmeric	colour yellow	pigment in turmeric (a spice)
140	chlorophyll	colour green	pigment in plants (also sold as a health supplement)
150	caramel	colour	cooked sugar
160a	carotene	colour	pigment in carrots and dark coloured fruits and vegetables
181	tannins	colour, emulsifier, stabiliser, thickener	tannins occur in tea
260	acetic acid	acidity regulator	vinegar
270	lactic acid	acidity regulator	yoghurt

300	ascorbic acid	antioxidant	vitamin C
307	α-Tocopherol	antioxidant	vitamin E
330	citric acid	antioxidant, acidity regulator	lemon juice
407	carageenan	thickener, gelling agent, stabiliser	seaweed
440	pectins	thickener, stabiliser, gelling agent	fruit
62	calcium glutamate	flavour enhancer	found in proteins (eg, cheese, sardines)

industry is out to kill us (which, at the very least, makes no business sense). Then there are people who genuinely experience food intolerance.

A small number of people can be sensitive to food additives and eating them can cause unpleasant symptoms—they can avoid the particular troublesome additive(s) by reading the food label. Because many food additives have long names, they are usually listed as numbers to save space. Food additive code numbers can be found on the food regulator websites.

As many food additives are the same or similar to naturally occurring food chemicals (see opposite), it is important you get expert advice before cutting foods or additives out of your diet. For example, the food additive MSG can cause the same symptoms as naturally glutamate-rich foods such as parmesan cheese, mushrooms, tomatoes and soy sauce.

Eating no food additives at all still may not solve food intolerance problems and you may be unnecessarily avoiding convenience foods you like. If you think some foods upset you, see a dietitian with experience in food intolerance.

KEY INFO All additives must be proven safe before being added to food products.

LONG STORY SHORT Food additives have allowed us to enjoy a variety of safe, enjoyable and appealing foods. If you're blaming food additives for your ill-health, you may be barking up the wrong tree. If you think you are sensitive to some foods, get expert help from a dietitian.

HUNGRY FOR MORE? See www.foodstandards.gov.au and www.codexalimentarius.net. If you think you may be sensitive to additives, check out www.sswahs.nsw.gov.au/RPA/Allergy.

⊙ Non-stick cookware is dangerous

Ask anyone who's had to scrape the burned-on remnants from a steel pan about non-stick cookware and they're bound to speak glowingly about the marvels of modern science. Health enthusiasts speak highly of non-stick cookware as a means by which to produce meals lower in fat. But really the biggest feature is that they are easy to clean. But what about those rumours about non-stick (Teflon-coated) pans creating toxic gases that can kill a pet bird?

Let's say first of all that using a non-stick pan for normal cooking is safe: you can relax, and there's no need to throw out your cookware. You just have to use the pan properly.

The problem is perfluorooctanoic acid (PFOA), a chemical used to bond the non-stick coating to the pan which, at very high temperatures, can kill pet birds and possibly cause flu-like symptoms. This is because, when non-stick cookware is heated to extremely high temperatures, the quality of the coating may begin to deteriorate, decompose and give off fumes. That's why it's important to follow the manufacturer's instructions and use non-stick pans on low or medium temperatures and not leave them unattended or allow them to get very hot without any food in them.

For stir-fries that do need very high heat, use a steel wok. For pan-frying a steak, you don't need the pan super hot. And if the non-stick coating gets scratched and starts to come off, it's time to get a new pan.

PFOA is being phased out by Dupont (the manufacturers of Teflon) and PFOA-free non-stick products are available. If you are concerned, check consumer publications such as *Which?* (www.which.co.uk), *Consumer Reports* (www.consumerreports. org) and *Choice* magazine (www.choice.com.au). These consumer watchdogs have had their eye on the non-stick problem for some time and can recommend the best brands to buy.

KEY INFO Various authorities have declared non-stick cookware safe; however, they should not be heated to very high temperatures because gases may be released from the surface. **LONG STORY SHORT** It's safe to use non-stick cookware but don't leave them empty on a very high heat, and keep the surface pristine by not using abrasive cleaners or metal utensils. **HUNGRY FOR MORE?** See www.epa.gov; Google Consumer Reports Q&A: Is cooking with nonstick pans bad for your health? And check out the Dupont website, which answers key questions about Teflon non-stick coatings: www.dupont.com/Teflon/en_US/products/safety/key_questions.html

▶ Aluminium pots cause Alzheimer's disease

Alzheimer's disease organisations and the majority of medical experts around the world agree that the link between aluminium (or aluminum in the USA) and Alzheimer's is far from proven. Despite the existence of seemingly plausible theories, there are far too many holes in them. Alzheimer's is a complex disease with multiple risk factors, suggesting a single cause is highly unlikely. Then there is the question of whether cooking in aluminium pots actually causes high aluminium levels in the body: this is unlikely too.

Too much aluminium in the body is toxic to the nervous system. Cases have been reported of some people with Alzheimer's having high concentrations of aluminium in their brain (but not all Alzheimer's sufferers). Aluminium is not well absorbed by the body—only around 1 per cent of what we ingest. People with kidney failure experience aluminium overload but don't have a higher risk of Alzheimer's.

There are small amounts of aluminium naturally present in foods and drinks such as milk, cheese, yeast extract (ie, Vegemite), tea, beer, olive oil and kiwifruit (just to name a few). Although it may seem weird that there is aluminium in food, in fact aluminium is everywhere—in water, soil and water. It is the third most abundant element in the Earth's crust. There is also aluminium in some food additives and an Acceptable Daily Intake (ADI) has been set to assess safety of exposure from these. It is also possible for trace amounts of aluminium to migrate from cookware and storage-ware into food; however, studies show the amounts are tiny. By far the biggest source of aluminium is antacid medications, used for the relief of reflux: these can increase aluminium intake by up to 100 times. Studies have failed to show any association between antacid use and Alzheimer's. Oh, and you've probably heard that deodorants contain aluminium: there's no association between deodorant use and Alzheimer's either.

Key info There is no proven link between Alzheimer's disease and aluminium. There is more naturally occurring aluminium in food than gets into food from cookware. Only around 1 per cent of aluminium we ingest is absorbed.

Long story short Most experts agree aluminium doesn't cause Alzheimer's.

Hungry for more? See http://alzheimers.org.uk.

⊙ GM foods are unsafe

In answering the question 'Are GM foods safe?' the World Health Organisation (WHO) says:

> Different GM organisms include different genes inserted in different ways. This means that individual GM foods and their safety should be assessed on a case-by-case basis and that it is not possible to make general statements on the safety of all GM foods. GM foods currently available on the international market have passed risk assessments and are not likely to present risks for human health. In addition, no effects on human health have been shown as a result of the consumption of such foods by the general population in the countries where they have been approved. Continuous use of risk assessments based on the Codex principles and, where appropriate, including post market monitoring, should form the basis for evaluating the safety of GM foods.

To date, GM foods have been eaten by millions of people around the world for nearly 20 years with no ill effects; indeed many GM foods are absolutely identical to their non-GM counterparts (it's just the plant that produced it that is genetically different).

However, depending on where you live, you may or may not find GM products on your supermarket shelves. GM produce does not have to be labelled in the USA. But it does in Europe where there is a great deal of consumer resistance to genetically modified foods and strict labelling laws and regulations are in place. In addition, supermarkets are very responsive to consumer concerns. For example, on their website, the UK food retailer Tesco says: 'Our policy on Genetically Modified (GM) foods is based on what you, our customers, have told us you want. And our research shows that UK customers don't want GM foods in our stores. So naturally we don't have any own-brand GM foods on our shelves and all of our organic animals are reared using non-GM feed.' You'll find similar promises on the websites of other supermarket chains.

People have been methodically improving crop plants through selective breeding for thousands of years, but this form of 'genetic modification' is very slow—it takes a long time to create desired characteristics in plants and animals. Modern GM is quick because it involves changing the genes of an animal or plant directly using molecular biology techniques. It is most commonly used to modify plants to be pest-, disease- or herbicide-resistant. For example, the most common GM plant is the soybean, which is resistant to glyphosate herbicide (weedkiller). This means farmers can spray the soybean crop for weeds but the soybean plants don't die as well. This GM crop was created by identifying the gene in a naturally herbicide-resistant soybean plant and splicing it into the DNA of another plant, which then becomes herbicide-resistant as well. In the case of GM cotton, the plant has been modified to produce a toxin that kills a common caterpillar which feasts on it, therefore dramatically reducing the need for pesticide.

Genetic modification techniques can be used to improve the nutritional profile of crops, such as rice with higher vitamin A content. Considering vitamin A deficiency is the main cause of blindness in developing countries, the benefits are obvious. In an increasingly hungry world grappling with the consequences of climate change, the potential to create beneficial characteristics in the food supply is great. Gosh, it all sounds good so far, so what's the catch?

Health concerns about GM crops are also related to a general discomfort about 'messing with nature' and the power of big business to control and dictate food production especially in poor countries. Large-scale industrialised agriculture concentrated in the hands of a few mega-corporations is an anathema to those who believe 'keeping it local' is the best way to ensure a healthy, equitable and sustainable food supply. They may have a point. Large agribusiness corporations actually patent the modified genes they develop and therefore 'own' food crops. The fact that farmers are not able to collect and re-plant seeds of GM—they have to buy new ones each season—seems unfair. In some cases farmers have been sued because their crop has become contaminated with a neighbour's GM variety. The United Nations has conceded that GM is not the magic bullet for feeding the world's hungry.

There is also the issue of GM crops cross-fertilising with wild plants and weeds surrounding them, creating herbicide-resistant 'superweeds'. The chances of this are thought to be very low but it has happened in an English field research trial of GM herbicide-resistant oilseed rape that cross-fertilised with a local weed called charlock and made that herbicide-resistant too. There have also been concerns raised about insects becoming resistant to the insect toxins produced by GM plants. Of course insect-resistance occurs with regular pesticide used on regular plants as well. There are problems to solve with GM crops, and scientists are keen to do more research.

The whole GM story seems like promising science that has been spoiled by corporate greed. Then again the big companies have invested a lot in GM development. I can't help thinking we need both global and local systems working in concert if we are to feed our rapidly growing world population and create fair food systems and food security for all. So far as 'messing with nature' goes, I don't buy it: we've been doing it for years.

KEY INFO GM foods must be approved by food safety authorities before use in the food supply. There is strong disagreement about the safety of GM foods. Other issues are the social, economic and environmental effects of the power yielded by giant multinational biotechnology companies.

LONG STORY SHORT To date there is no conclusive evidence that any GM food approved by regulatory authorities is harmful. GM technology has the capacity to benefit human health and improve food supply productivity and sustainability but there are still big issues around equity and corporate greed. Consumers can't decide whether or not they want to eat GM foods in countries where there are no or inadequate labelling requirements. Organic foods are GM-free.

HUNGRY FOR MORE? See WHO's 20 questions on GM foods www.who.int/foodsafety/publications/biotech/20questions/en/ and www.biotechnologyonline.gov.au/foodag/gmlabelling.html; read both sides of the argument on www.agbioworld.org (pro-GM) and www.ucsusa.org (anti-GM). Also search for 'GM foods' on your food regulators website eg www.foodstandards.gov.au or www.efsa.europa.eu or www.fda.gov

⊙ Foods you cook yourself are always healthier

Food and cooking are back in fashion. This cultural shift is punctuated by the phenomena of *Jamie Oliver's Food Revolution*, the ratings behemoth of *Masterchef*, amazing sales of cookbooks and the endless buffet of celebrity chefs, cooking shows and food magazines. I hope this has had some positive impacts on the community at large. I've heard many stories of children being inspired to cook by watching *Masterchef* on TV, and families becoming inspired to cook more at home for fun. The question is, are we eating any healthier?

One reason why the food and cooking trend may not have traction on our path to health is that many of us are just looking rather than doing it—the reason premium cookbooks are known as 'gastro-porn'! Meals eaten away from home continue to grow, and our love affair with fast food shows no sign of slowing down.

Unfortunately, many of the recipes we see are not healthy. Celebrity chefs are famous for their liberal use of fatty meat, butter, cream and salt. Most demonstrate what I call 'special occasion' or 'sometimes' food, yet this is rarely pointed out. Ingredients used in an episode of *Masterchef* experience massive sales increases after the show goes to air, so it appears quite a few of us cook what they cook.

But even if we don't actually cook the recipes: what about role modelling? Celebrity chefs have attained rock-star status but it is a lost opportunity when vegetables hardly feature on the 'restaurant-quality' meals presented and many recipes contain an entire day's worth of salt in a single dish. When the food prepared is more approachable, it draws on peasant origins designed for toiling in the fields with large portions and all the trimmings; hardly suitable for our sedentary lifestyles. If cooking on the TV and celebrity chef cookbooks are any indication of what we're eating at home, it is little wonder we're in trouble with diet-related disease. See *The joy of cooking ... too much* (on page 245).

Packets or love?

Many people speak ill of foods in packets like chocolate bars but feel good about whipping up a chocolate mud cake from scratch and eating a generous slice, although, on any objective measure of kilojoules and saturated fat, the home-made treat is worse. It is easy to criticise a fast-food burger but somehow Jamie's steak and cheese pie with all-butter pastry has a health halo. I've done a small study on the types of fats used in magazine recipes and it's little wonder high cholesterol levels are so common.

'But what about the love?' I hear you ask. The love in home cooking cannot be measured, but it still doesn't counteract a diet of excess—although you may die happy with a face full of pie!

A good cook used to know about balance, moderation, variety, seasons and providing nourishing meals on a budget. The same knowledge and skills are needed today, and add environmentally sustainable and extra-healthy to the list. Much of what we see of cooking in the media has a different focus. If more home cooking is to help our wellbeing, we have to see more about healthy eating in our infotainment. Or switch off and take lessons from grandma.

KEY INFO Most recipes on TV cooking shows (and in gourmet food magazines) are 'special occasion' foods with loads of saturated fat and salt and not enough essential foods such as vegetables, wholegrains and legumes. And they tend to be expensive.

LONG STORY SHORT Just because you cook it yourself, doesn't mean it's healthy. It depends on what you cook, how you cook it and how much you eat.

HUNGRY FOR MORE? See *Food additives are harmful*, page 231. For healthy recipes and solid advice check out my other books *Eat To Beat Cholesterol*, *Heart Food* and *Belly Busting for Blokes* or join healthy cooking classes in your area.

The joy of cooking ... too much

Eating out is often blamed as being one of the key culprits for gaining weight, but a letter published in the *Annals of Internal Medicine*, suggests that what we do in our own homes may be just as bad. In the study, the researchers found recipes for four, that would have served around seven people in 1936.

Examining 18 'classic' recipes found in seven editions of the 'classic' *The Joy of Cooking* since it was first published in 1936 until the 2006 update, Dr Brian Wansink and Dr Collin Payne found that in 17 of the 18 recipes the average calories per serving jumped 63 per cent in 70 years—that's from about 268 calories (1125 kJ) per serving in 1936 to about 436 calories (1831 kJ) in 2006.

In analysing just the calorie density of the recipes—the total amount of calories, regardless of serving size—the foods in the 2006 edition had 37 per cent more calories than the 18 recipes did in the 1936 edition. Similar increases were found in other classics such as the *Better Homes and Gardens Cook Book*.

Speaking to Susan Lang of the *Cornell Chronicle*, Dr Wansink said: 'This jump in calories was influenced by both changes in ingredients—usually increases in fat and sugar—and changes in serving size. Family size has gotten smaller, but calorie content and portion sizes have gotten bigger'. The researchers cite beef stroganoff as an example. In the 1997 edition, the recipe called for 3 tablespoons of sour cream (that's less than ¼ cup). The 2006 edition calls for 1 whole cup. The study also found that some of the added calories came from substituting ingredients, such as extra meat instead of vegetables.

⏵ Healthy food is cheaper

Cooking fresh foods from scratch tends to be healthier (although not always) and can cost less because you are not paying a premium for someone else doing the work. However, this is not always the case. Saving money by cooking from scratch relies on high-level skills in planning, budgeting, shopping, cooking and all-round food management. It also relies on time: a resource many people say they don't have.

Some unhealthy food has become too cheap. There are vast economies of scale within big food corporations and marketing strategies that can make poor food choices cost less. For example, a fast-food 'family meal deal' can be very cost competitive because large fast-food companies actually make a small loss on promotional items in order to hook new customers or boost sales volumes. The logistics of getting processed shelf-stable foods to you is so much easier because they don't go off. In Australia we are importing a growing amount of processed foods from Asia that are cheap because of lower production costs; however, much of it is nutritionally poor.

Modern industrialised food production has also led us to expect to pay very little for food. Most cheap food does not account for the environmental, health and social costs they impose and many of us are unaware of these hidden costs. For example, the environmental degradation and biodiversity loss of intensive agriculture, the poor farmers forced into hardship by retailer price wars, the exploitation of child labour in developing countries and the health costs of easily accessible 'junk food'.

There are too many caveats to the notion that healthy food is cheaper for it to hold true any more. For a family with limited income, filling bellies for the least cost is paramount and the temptation to buy unhealthy choices is great. Add to this the heavy promotion of less nutritious foods, a decline of cooking skills plus time-stress, and it is little wonder we take the cheap and fast option. Unfortunately, the most disadvantaged in our society eat a poorer diet and suffer the consequences of higher rates of diet-related disease.

The challenge for the future is shifting to a more sustainable food system that supports the environment as well as the health and wellbeing of people while still keeping the food industry viable to sustain livelihoods. If you can afford better food, please buy it: it's a great investment in your health and a better world.

Key info Food is now big business and can be produced cheaply; however, it is not always the healthiest or most sustainable food. The challenge is to make healthy food affordable and accessible for those who are on low incomes and most at risk of diet-related disease.

Long story short Cheap food has hidden environmental, social and health costs. Healthy, sustainable food does cost more but you can save money and eat better by gaining skills in food planning, shopping and cooking.

Hungry for more? Visit www.moneysavingmeals.com.au. See *Foods you cook yourself are always healthier*, page 243 ; *Frozen foods are less nutritious*, page 263; *Food additives are harmful*, page 231.

Tips to save money on healthy food

- Buy fresh produce that is in season when it costs less.
- Use cheaper meat cuts and trim before cooking or skim the fat after cooking and cooling.
- Use less meat and fill out meals with legumes (such as lentils, chickpeas and cooked dried beans).
- Learn to cook!
- Buy foods on sale, but only if you will eat them within their 'use-by' date.
- Plan meals for the week so you only buy what you need.
- Reduce waste by freezing leftovers for another day.
- Be selective in the processed foods you buy and look for products lower in saturated fat and salt.

▶ I take medication so I don't need to watch what I eat

Have you heard of people who say they can carry on eating badly because 'the pills will fix it'. I've heard this quite a bit in relation to medication that lowers cholesterol.

Let's start with cholesterol pills. These medications, called statins, make the liver produce less cholesterol so the level in the blood goes down.

What they don't do is provide help with any of the many other risk factors we know increase the risk of heart attack. They do nothing to: reduce fat from the belly (or anywhere for that matter); reduce blood glucose levels; reduce blood pressure, or to increase the good HDL (high-density lipoproteins) cholesterol levels that protect against heart disease. They do nothing to reduce the oxidation of cholesterol that's already there (which contributes to hardening of the arteries), or reduce the stiffness of blood vessels (called arterial compliance), or reduce blood triglyceride levels (the other nasty blood fat that increases risk). They also do nothing to reduce the tendency of the blood to clot (blood clots cause heart attacks and some kinds of stroke) or to maintain a steady regular heart beat that prevents sudden cardiac death. And of course that is to say nothing of the potential for side effects, the most common being muscle pain (myalgia).

And then there's the prickly issue of the cost, which in the UK, Australia and New Zealand is subsidised by the taxpayer.

Unbelievably, a study has been done to examine the effect of giving statins with fast food to reduce harm. Researchers assessed the risk posed by excessive fat and trans-fat consumption in a daily 200g (7oz) fast-food burger with cheese and a small milkshake, and the effect of a daily dose of statin drug. They found (as far as they could estimate) they neatly cancelled each other out. They concluded that statin therapy can neutralise the cardiovascular risk from harmful dietary choices and perhaps fast-food outlets might offer statins 'on the side' with their meals. Oh dear—what planet are these researchers on?

This article was published in a mainstream peer-reviewed *American Journal of Cardiology* and is not a joke. Where to start? Firstly, trying to fix bad food choices with pharmaceuticals is like saying we might as well colonise another planet since we've wrecked this one. It's the ultimate white flag, the end of the line. It is utterly defeatist, except for the obvious boon to the bottom lines of drug companies. Secondly, it is too simplistic to quantify the health impact of a poor food choice by only considering cholesterol levels. It ignores the other risk factors statins do not influence, and the power of protective foods that statins can never hope to reach. What consumers are after is natural whole foods with less additives, not more.

The fast-food chains will think it's a stupid idea as well. For one, they would have to admit that consuming their food on a daily basis is harmful. It is currently not possible to add drugs to food—mercifully, they have been kept separate. I do not foresee this changing in the future. You think genetically modified (GM) foods have caused a fuss? It is nothing compared with the backlash we'd see against adding drugs to food. Now, can we get on with doing some useful research?

---

5 easy ways to beat cholesterol-lowering drugs

---

1.   Eat porridge or muesli for breakfast.
2.   Switch from butter to 'plant-sterol' enriched margarine spreads.
3.   Eat a handful of nuts a day.
4.   Switch to low-fat milk.
5.   Use lean meat or trim the fat.

KEY INFO Cholesterol-lowering drugs only affect cholesterol; there are many other risk factors they do not influence.

LONG STORY SHORT Drugs can never take the place of a healthy diet and lifestyle

HUNGRY FOR MORE? See www.heartuk.org.uk and search 'portfolio diet'; also *GM foods are unsafe*, page 239.

▶ Ancient grains are healthier than modern

Ancient grains such as spelt, chia, amaranth and quinoa are fashionable at the moment, albeit hard to get and more expensive. The rising popularity of these old-world grains is great because variety in the diet, and variety in agricultural production, is good for us and good for the environment. However, there are plenty of grains and seeds that are less trendy, but more available, affordable and also nutritious.

Spelt bread is sold at a premium, but what it is? Spelt is an age-old variety of wheat, and spelt bread has a medium GI, although some multigrain varieties make it into the low category. Although spelt is advertised as 'easier to digest', and 'suitable for those allergic to wheat', it is certainly not suitable for those with a wheat allergy or coeliac disease and there is little published evidence for easier digestability.

Some people attribute all sorts of health problems and digestive symptoms to eating wheat, and many will get relief from varying the grains they eat. However, those with symptoms often have a more complex food chemical (natural and added) sensitivity problem rather than intolerance to wheat (See *Wheat is hard to digest and makes you bloated*, page 159). But variety is the spice of life, so vary your diet from wheat thrice daily with, for example, oats for breakfast, rice salad for lunch, and barley hotpot or a polenta-based dish for dinner.

Chia is a new player in the game of 'what grain is that?' Related to the mint family, chia is the seed of *Salvia hispanica* and, as the name suggests, originates from Latin America. It is rich in omega-3 and omega-6 fatty acids, protein and fibre—qualities similar to other seeds. Traditionally it was used to make porridge and bread by the Mayans and Aztecs. You can buy chia seeds online, but they are mostly used as an ingredient in food products. People allergic to sesame seeds and mustard seeds are advised to avoid chia. If you can't get hold of chia products, or you can't afford their premium pricing, try other seeds such as sunflower, pumpkin and linseeds, which have similar nutritional properties.

Amaranth has been growth for thousands of years and was eaten by the Aztecs. It is also gluten-free and provides a welcome 'starch-change' to rice and potato on the dinner plates of those with diagnosed coeliac disease. It is slightly higher in protein than other grains at 14 per cent (uncooked form) and the plant is very hardy. You can find amaranth breakfast cereal in health food stores and some supermarkets, priced at a premium. Puffed or 'popped' amaranth has a high GI. If you're looking to eat something healthy and different for breakfast, try making your own cereal using a variety of puffed grains (corn, millet, brown rice, buckwheat), rolled oats, chopped nuts and dried fruit—variety in a bowl. Store your designer cereal in a cool place in an airtight container.

Quinoa (pronounced keen-wa) is grown in the Andes Mountains and was consumed by ancient Incas, cementing South America as the hotspot origin for ancient grains. Like other grains it is high in carbohydrate (68%), low in fat (4.8%) and moderate in protein (12%), and it is gluten-free as well. You cook it similarly to rice—1 cup dry quinoa to 2 cups water. It has a low GI when cooked, cooled and re-heated, which fits in nicely with cooking a large batch and freezing in meal-size portions for convenience. I cooked some quinoa recently, and served it in place of pasta with a vegetables and butter beans in tomato-based sauce. I enjoyed the tiny grains, but my beloved was less keen on the 'funny rice'. Sometimes it's hard being a food pioneer, but it won't stop me!

Key info Ancient grains are becoming more popular but are often expensive. These trendy grains are nutritionally similar to commoner and cheaper ones.

LONG STORY SHORT Old and new grains are good for you, and wholegrains are best.

HUNGRY FOR MORE? See www.wholegrainscouncil.org.

⊙ Some foods are aphrodisiacs

If aphrodisiac foods are those that get you in the mood for love (improve your libido), then the hype surrounding foods such as oysters may be more folklore and fun than scientific fact (aphrodisiologists will disagree of course!). Human desire is rather more psychological than nutritional. It is probably the care and devotion involved in sourcing, preparing and sharing special foods, and the sensuality of eating them that set the scene for love, rather than the foods themselves. However, if the spirit is willing, the equipment must also be in order and this is where food can help.

Physical problems in the bedroom are far more common in men, and erectile dysfunction (ED) is the usual culprit. In a study of more than 31,000 men in the US (The Health Professionals Follow-up Study), moderate-to-severe erectile dysfunction was reported by 12 per cent of men younger than 59 years; 22 per cent of men aged 60 to 69; and 30 per cent of men older than 69 years. So what can be done to avoid this distressing problem?

The blood vessels 'down south' become blocked just as they do in the heart because of atherosclerosis. Erectile dysfunction is an early warning sign of high cholesterol and cardiovascular disease. It is also much more likely in men with the metabolic syndrome and diabetes. Young men take note: maintaining a healthy weight, lowering LDL (bad) blood cholesterol levels, maintaining ideal blood pressures and NOT smoking are important ways to look after your blood vessels and keep you loving longer. And the same principles apply to reducing the problem once it occurs. Studies show that lifestyle changes such as lowering LDL (bad) cholesterol, losing weight, and exercising can enhance sexual function by up to 70 per cent! So, a healthy diet and lifestyle can keep your heart beating strongly in more ways than one.

Oh, and gentlemen: surveys of women suggest if you help with the housework she'll be more receptive to your amorous advances, so don't forget to help with the washing up!

Food for love

- Colour his world with plenty of different types of vegetables and fruits
- Make him whole again with plenty of wholegrains, such as oats, wholewheat breads, pasta and breakfast cereals, barley and brown rice
- Feed him like a Greek god with Mediterranean fare such as legumes, fish, fruit and nuts
- Grease his wheels by replacing butter, cream, pastries and fast foods with healthy oils and trans-free margarine spreads based on sunflower, canola, soybean and olive oils.
- Give him longer lasting energy with lower GI foods such as reduced-fat milk and yoghurt, grainy breads, pasta, legumes and fruits.

KEY INFO Libido is complicated and more in the mind than in the food we eat. Erectile dysfunction (impotence) is common but a healthy lifestyle can help prevent and manage it.

LONG STORY SHORT Aphrodisiac foods may have more to do with creating the mood than with the food itself.

HUNGRY FOR MORE? See www.mayoclinic.com/health/erectile-dysfunction and www.andrologyaustralia.org (erectile dysfunction).

ⓟ Organic food is better for you

Organic farming is a more natural and sustainable way of producing food and it respects the environment by prioritising the health of the soil, air, water, animals and people. Organic food is produced without synthetic (man-made) fertilisers and pesticides. Organic farms compost and recycle waste, which is a valuable and renewable source of nutrients.

Whether organic foods contain more nutrients is controversial. While the organic industry continues to say organic food contains higher nutrient levels, several large scientific reviews have concluded there is not enough evidence to say for sure, and many studies show no difference. For some foods, the research has not yet been done. The US Department of Agriculture (USDA) cannot say organically produced food is more nutritious than conventionally grown produce. The UK Food Standards Agency (FSA) and Food Standards Australia and New Zealand (FSANZ) say there is insufficient evidence to conclude organic food is more nutritious.

Organic food is more expensive and this is a barrier to people on low incomes. I'd rather they eat 'two fruit and five veg' of the conventional kind rather than having to skimp on organic because of the cost.

And a word on organic agriculture: I'm all for it. However, there simply isn't enough organics to feed everyone and it does not have the potential to take over from conventional agriculture to meet our growing food needs. As one professor of sustainable agriculture said to me, we're going to need something new—a kind of hybrid approach—that combines the best of both systems to feed the world.

Then there is the issue of chemical residues in conventionally produced food. Total Diet Surveys (TDS) conducted every few years in Australia show time after time that exposure to chemical residues in food is low and well within internationally recognised limits. The US Food and Drug Administration (USFDA) says the same. However, in a surprising admission, the US President's Cancer Panel recommended people choose organic produce— or wash conventional produce—to limit their chemical exposure because it was unconvinced of their safety: it believes environmental cancer triggers are underestimated.

KEY INFO There is no conclusive evidence that organic food is more nutritious than conventionally produced food, but chemical residues are lower. Organic food production has environmental sustainability advantages.

LONG STORY SHORT Organic food is a great choice for the environment if you can afford it. If you can't don't worry: just aim to eat your two fruit and five veggies a day for good health and wash produce before eating.

HUNGRY FOR MORE? See www.bfa.com.au; www.food. gov.uk/foodindustry/farmingfood/organicfood; www. fruitsandveggiesmatter.gov; and www.gofor2and5.com.au. Also *Our food is toxic*, page 267.

⊙ Food should be thrown out after its 'best-before' date

Confusion over date labelling on packaged foods means that good food gets wasted and ends up in the bin because many people think 'use-by' and 'best-before' dates are the same thing.

Think of best-before as a guide to food **quality**. Don't automatically bin food once it has passed its 'best-before' date. It should be perfectly safe to eat, providing it has been properly stored at home and at the supermarket but it may not taste as good. You generally find 'best-before' dates on canned foods, cereals, biscuits, sauces, chocolate, sugar, flour and frozen foods.

Ronni Kahn, founder of an organisation that distributes surplus food from retailers and restaurants to needy people, says 'best-before' date labels encourage consumers to throw away good food and buy more. 'My granny didn't know about "best-before" dates. She smelt the food. If it was good, we ate it. If it wasn't, we didn't,' Kahn said. She makes a good point that we ought to be more frugal and less wasteful with our food.

'Use-by' dates are about food **safety** and you will find them on perishables such as milk, sliced ham, some smallgoods and shaved meats, fish and dairy products. Foods can't be sold after that date. If it's a carton of milk in your fridge and you don't want to waste it, smell it. It is pretty obvious when milk is off. The same can't be said for other foods so it's best to err on the side of caution and 'if in doubt, throw it out'. Of course, you can prevent throwing food away by only buying what you need and storing it properly. Don't forget you can freeze milk, leftovers, bread, fresh meat, chicken and fish.

But don't just rely on dates. Look at the packaging itself. One of my favourite resources, the brilliant Better Health Channel reminds us that: 'Foods can become spoiled well before their "use-by" or "best before" date, either because their packaging has been damaged or they weren't stored properly at the supermarket. When buying foods, check for dents, leaks and tears in the packaging—if you can see any sign of damage, don't buy the product, as it might be contaminated with bacteria. Many products, such as dairy foods, need to be kept at a low temperature to avoid spoilage. Don't buy any foods that need to be chilled or frozen if they are sitting on unrefrigerated shelves, or stacked in overfilled fridges.'

KEY INFO Providing it has been stored properly and the package isn't damaged, food is OK to eat after it's 'best-before' date. It may be unsafe to eat food past it's 'use-by' date.

LONG STORY SHORT Whatever the date stamp, check the label. Check the package. To prevent waste, don't buy too much and store food properly.

HUNGRY FOR MORE? See Better Health Channel: 'Food use-by and best-before dates'.

⊙ Microwave cooking myths

There are many myths and misconceptions about microwave ovens, but it doesn't seem to deter sales—they are one of the most popular home appliances. Here are some common myths.

You lose nutrients when you cook food in the microwave

To preserve their nutritional goodness, the best cooking methods for vegetables are microwaving, stir-frying and steaming. Avoid boiling as you will be pouring vitamins down the drain along with the cooking water. I personally love vegetables cooked in the microwave as the rapid cooking in very little water ensures they keep their lovely colour as well as those vital vitamins and minerals.

Microwaves cook food from the inside out

The 'microwaves' actually work on the outer layers of food, penetrating to a depth of about 5cm. They agitate the water molecules in the food—this creates heat which cooks the food.

You can get cold spots (where bacteria can thrive)

This is why it is important to stir foods such as soups and casseroles you are cooking or heating in the microwave, or leave dishes (like roasts or quiches) to stand to let the heat penetrate. Tip: for even cooking, it helps to cut food into similar sized chunks. Smaller chunks cook more evenly than larger ones.

Microwaving food exposes you to radiation

As soon as the oven is OFF there are no microwaves in the oven or the food. Radiation leaks are possible if the door is damaged or doesn't seal properly. In most cases, leaks are too small to cause significant health risk.

KEY INFO Microwave ovens are convenient, time-saving appliances manufactured to high safety standards

Long story short Microwave ovens cook foods faster than conventional methods, making them handy time savers. **Hungry for more?** See Better Health Channel: 'Microwave ovens—safety issues'.

▶ Frozen foods are less nutritious than fresh

The usual suspect for this popular myth is vegetables. And it's probably true: nothing is going to be more nutritious and tasty than freshly picked vegetables from the garden served the same day.

These days, frozen vegetables come close. They are picked at their peak and snap-frozen within hours of picking, which makes them a very nutritious option. In fact, frozen peas will retain more of their vitamins and minerals than will the shelled pre-packed peas on the greengrocer's shelf. Add to this their convenience: the processor has done the boring prepping for us—shelling the peas, slicing the beans, cutting the broccoli into even-sized florets and dicing the carrots. It's like having home help!

Frozen foods also make it possible for us to serve our favourite vegetables and berries year round at affordable prices.

There tends to be much less waste too. Whereas fresh vegetables don't always last the week in the crisper drawer and so get thrown out or on the compost, the packs of frozen peas or beans or corn wait for weeks in the freezer for their chance to make it to your dinner plate to help you get your five serves a day.

Perhaps the real question to ask here is: how fresh are the fresh vegetables on sale in your produce store? Many will have been shipped long distances before even making it into the store and finally your plate. It's a bit of a trek during which time nutrient levels can fall.

Frozen meals can be a healthy and convenient option too—they sure beat most takeouts. Pass on the pizza and pies and head for ready-made balanced meals in the freezer section of your supermarket. Look for the healthy cues on the label like 'low fat', 'lean' and endorsements from health bodies. Check the nutrition label to find the lowest for sodium and saturated fat.

Get into the freezing act yourself. Cook a little extra and freeze the leftovers. This reduces food waste, saves money and helps you to eat well when you're busy.

KEY INFO Keeping frozen vegetables in the freezer helps you get your five serves a day—and frozen berries make a sensational dessert and are handy for making smoothies or topping your cereal in the morning.

LONG STORY SHORT Frozen foods can be healthy, nutritious timesavers.

HUNGRY FOR MORE? See www.frozenfoodinfo.com.au (food industry site).

⊙ Coffee sobers you up

Sorry, the only thing that sobers you up if you have drunk too much alcohol is **time**. It's not a question of having a cup of strong black coffee to wake you up, nor a cold shower. It's a question of getting the alcohol out of your body. And that takes time. If you have a large glass (250ml/8fl oz) wine, you need to allow about three hours for your body to break down the alcohol. So imagine how long a night on the town takes …

In fact, there are no hard and fast rules about how long the alcohol will stay in your body—it depends on your age and weight, whether you're male or female, what sort of metabolism you have, how much food you've eaten, the type of alcohol over what period of time and whether you are on any medication.

Downing a mug of coffee may be the worst thing you can do, according to a Temple University study (in mice) published in *Behavioural Neuroscience*. In the laboratory, caffeine made 'drunk' mice more alert but did not reverse the learning problems caused by alcohol, including their ability to avoid things they should have known could hurt them.

The same results have been found in people who combine caffeine-loaded energy drinks with alcohol: the caffeine makes them more alert but their judgement is still impaired by the alcohol. In effect, the caffeine-alcohol combination makes you feel like you can, but actually you can't: the potential for injury and misadventure is obvious.

The good news is that another study (in rats this time) has shown that a cup of coffee and an aspirin may help with the sore head the next day.

KEY INFO Coffee may make you feel more alert when you have drunk too much—but it doesn't help you make better decisions or drive safely.

LONG STORY SHORT Only time breaks down alcohol in the body.

HUNGRY FOR MORE? See http://rethinkingdrinking.niaaa.nih.gov and www.drinkaware.co.uk/facts/factsheets/alcohol-and-your-health.

⏵ Our food is toxic

This statement is absurd as it implies there is harm from eating any food in any amount. However, there are issues of chemical residue exposure from the food we eat and the extent of the contamination depends on where you live and what you eat. Even so, the fear about synthetic chemicals in food far outweighs the actual harm.

Many countries, including the UK, Canada, the USA, Australia and New Zealand, carry out studies called the Total Diet Survey (TDS) every few years to measure exposure to chemical residues and contaminants such as fertilisers, pesticides and industrial chemicals. In Australia and New Zealand the food supply has a 'clean and green' reputation internationally. And there is analytical support for this: TDS results repeatedly show that the exposure is low and does not represent a risk to health. Sure, there are baddies in there, but the amounts are small enough not to be dangerous. A more recent concern is increases in imported foods from countries with less stringent rules and regulations: only a small proportion is actually tested. In the US, the results of the FDA's TDS, which are available on their website, indicate levels are within the acceptable limits set by the World Health Organisation.

Having said all this, there are toxic chemicals in our bodies from the air, water and food. For example, The US Centers for Disease Control have detected pesticides in the blood and urine of 96 per cent of a sample of 5000 adults. Health and environmental advocates say large agribusiness has too much influence on assessing the safety of chemicals used to produce food. Single surveys do not tell the whole story and of course foods with high levels are occasionally found. A *Choice* magazine (Australia) survey in 2008 found three out of 31 samples of strawberries purchased in Sydney contained pesticide levels above the Maximum Residue Limit (MRL). Real questions have

The importance of food safety

The main way food can become toxic is if dangerous 'bugs' such as bacteria, viruses and fungi are allowed to grow in it. This is not due to how the food is grown, but how well we look after it. When we don't, the results can be tragic. An outbreak of *Escherichia coli* bacteria in fresh bean sprouts caused the death of 22 people and left more than 2000 sick (including 600 in intensive care) in Europe in 2011.

Many cases of food poisoning (called food-borne illness) are caused by poor food handling in the home. To ensure you don't poison your family or your guests:

- Wash hands regularly, especially when preparing food.
- Wash fruits and vegetables before eating.
- Ensure your kitchen and food utensils are kept very clean using hot soapy water.
- Keep hot foods hot and cold foods cold—don't let food sit around at room temperature.
- Prevent cross-contamination between raw meat, fish and chicken with cooked or raw ready-to-eat foods by using separate knives and chopping boards or washing very well in hot soapy water in between.

For more information go to www.food. gov. uk or www. foodsafety.asn.au.

---

been raised as to whether the enforcement of MRLs by state and territory authorities is adequate.

For both health and environmental reasons, we should be pushing for minimal use of potentially harmful chemicals in our food. We probably need some chemicals—as any home gardener will attest—to maintain productive yields to feed a rapidly growing population, but we need to be smarter about it. Choosing organic foods is an obvious choice to limit your exposure because they are grown without the use of synthetic fertilisers, pesticides or herbicides. Washing fresh conventional produce also helps.

You may have heard of the 'dirty dozen': fruits and vegetables with the highest levels of pesticides in the USA. This list was put together by the Environmental Working Group (EWG, a not-for-profit organisation) and makes for worrying reading: the iconic apple topped the list.

1. apples
2. celery
3. strawberries
4. peaches
5. spinach
6. nectarines (imported)
7. grapes (imported)
8. sweet bell peppers (capsicum)
9. potatoes
10. blueberries
11. lettuce
12. kale/collard greens

Of course, grower groups dispute the significance of the findings, saying the issue has been blown out of proportion. They may have a point: even the EWG says we're better off eating conventionally grown produce for their health benefits than none at all. But considering the highest risk of toxic chemicals in our food is to children and pregnant women, many young families are taking a cautionary approach and choosing to buy organic.

Key info Food is a source of environmental exposure to potentially harmful chemicals (as are air and water). Pregnant women and children are most vulnerable to harmful effects. Studies by food safety authorities indicate that generally levels are within acceptable limits.

Long story short Although we should strive for reduced use of potentially harmful chemicals to grow and produce food, levels are low and considered safe. Buying organic food significantly reduces your exposure.

Hungry for more? See *Avoid fish because of mercury content*, page 271; *Food additives are harmful*, page 231; www.foodstandards. gov.au—search Australian Total Diet Survey; www.fda.gov— search Total Diet Study; and Environment Working Group www.ewg.org.

⏵ Avoid fish because of mercury content

Fish is a highly nutritious food and a great source of the essential long-chain omega-3 fatty acids we need for optimal brain and heart health. Eating fish is important—many people do not get enough of these omega-3s. The issue of mercury in fish and seafood is a real fly in the ointment!

The problem is methyl mercury, a heavy metal that is toxic in large amounts. Excessive mercury consumption is particularly risky for pregnant women and children because it can damage the developing baby and adversely affect children's development. Although mercury exists naturally in our oceans, it is also an industrial pollutant. Mercury ends up in fish because the mercury in the ocean gets concentrated as you go up the marine food chain: little fish get eaten by bigger fish, which then get eaten by bigger fish again, which are then eaten by the biggest fish. The end result is top-of-the-food-chain fish are carrying unwanted chemical baggage: this is called bioaccumulation. Eating these predators of the sea increases our mercury levels when we eat too much of them.

However, mercury causes problems only at high levels, only in vulnerable people—and not all types of fish have high levels. Most of us can still eat the recommended two fish meals a week, provided you don't choose the very high mercury species. Pregnant women and young children need to be the most cautious. It isn't difficult to eat two serves a week of fish with low mercury content because there are lots that are just fine.

Mercury levels and fish species vary around the world—you should check with your local food safety authority about what fish you might need to limit. The high-level species tend to be larger predatory fish that live a long time. You needn't worry about canned tuna, salmon, mackerel and sardines because these are smaller and have a short lifespan, but do take care with shark (flake), billfish (eg, marlin) and catfish.

KEY INFO For most people, mercury in fish and shellfish is harmless. Only fish with high levels of mercury need to be limited, and mostly for pregnant and breastfeeding women and young children.

LONG STORY SHORT Eat fish and seafood regularly because they are highly nutritious. Check your local food safety authority for local fish recommendations.

HUNGRY FOR MORE? See www.food.gov.uk; www.fda.gov—search for methylmercury; and www.foodstandards.gov.au. Also see *Our food is toxic*, page 267, and *Flaxseed oil is as good as fish oil*, page 196.

⏵ Foods labelled natural are healthier

'Natural' is one of the most popular claims made for food and drink products around the world. But are we always getting something healthier when we buy foods with 'natural' on the label?

The term 'natural' on food labels is not regulated and therefore is open to interpretation. Research has found consumer expectations of 'natural' are different to those of food companies.

In terms of adverse nutrients—such as saturated fat and sodium—'natural' does not mean healthier. Salt, butter, lard and cream are natural, but they are disastrous to our health when eaten in significant amounts, and surveys show we are still eating too much of these. Organic claims carry high credibility with consumers, but may not actually deliver the health benefits expected.

Although organic food is better for the environment, it is not necessarily better for your health. An organic muffin made with white flour, butter and sugar is still a high-kilojoule, high-saturated fat snack with poor nutritional value—the addition of blueberries does little to redeem it. I once read 'organic crystallised sugar cane juice' on the label of a so-called 'health bar'—a classic case of sugar dressed up as natural, dressed up as healthy. Similarly, I have encountered an organic 'health bar' made with white flour, butter, sugar and oats, with enough saturated fat to exceed the entire day's maximum and as many kilojoules as an entire meal. Another obvious example is 'natural' confectionary, which contains as much sugar and calories as the regular stuff, and offers no health benefit for most people (see *Food additives are harmful*, page 231).

Is our hankering for 'natural' foods a sign of disillusionment about the modern pace of life and our complex food environment? Perhaps 'natural' is a word that promises deliverance from the time and stress of interpreting nutrition labels? This same simple rationale is behind traffic light labelling: red means unhealthy and green means healthy, right? Well, no, not always, and so much depends on the individual dietary context, frequency and amount you eat. Like a lot of areas in nutrition, the simple way doesn't always guarantee the best way, and can create collateral damage. If we are to make the best of our sophisticated food supply, we must read and understand the nutrition information on our food. A good first step is relinquishing our desperate grip on the 'natural' claim as a healthy signpost. Sometimes 'natural' is anything but healthy. Oh, and eat more fresh foods without labels—much food goodness needs no advertising.

KEY INFO The word 'natural' on a label does not automatically mean healthy: it is open to interpretation.

LONG STORY SHORT 'Natural' claims on foods mean very little. To find healthier foods, check the ingredients list and nutrition information panel on the label, and try eating more fresh foods that don't need labels.

HUNGRY FOR MORE? See www.fsis.usda.gov/OPPDE/larc/Policies/ Labeling_Policy_Book_082005.pdf—look up 'n' for natural); www.foodsafety.gov; www.nhs.uk and search for 'food safety'; or search for 'food descriptor guidelines' at www.accc.gov.au.

PART 5

Old wives' tales

⊙ An apple a day

There's some truth in this one. Apples are rich in soluble fibre, vitamin C and a group of antioxidants called flavonoids. They deserve star billing for helping to protect against some cancers, type 2 diabetes and asthma, keep the heart healthy and boost the immune system. Red, green or somewhere in-between, eat apples for enjoyment and for their many health benefits. They have a low GI (38) and a relatively low energy density, or kilojoules per gram. In effect, they fill you up without being fattening. Fresh is best—skin and all—to maximise nutrients and phytochemicals; however, variety is the spice of life and apples are delicious baked, dried, canned and juiced. Apple juice usually has the goodness of the fibre removed, so pick whole apples rather than juice most of the time.

In a world where eating for health can become complicated and costly, it's good to know that something so naturally sweet and filling will help you enjoy a lifetime of health benefits.

⊙ Carrots help you see in the dark

This is actually a myth—but when it comes to good vision, there's a vital carrot connection. Here's what happens. Carrots are rich in beta-carotene, which our bodies convert to vitamin A and which we need to maintain normal vision. A deficiency in vitamin A produces night blindness. In fact, carrots are so rich in beta-carotene that the whole golden 'carotenoid family' was named after them. A couple of tips:

- the deeper the colour the more beta-carotene
- we absorb more beta-carotene from cooked carrots than raw.

And there's more. They also have some lycopene and lutein, which help protect and preserve your eyes from cataracts and macular degeneration.

Grate and add carrots to salads and sandwiches, cut into sticks for dips or snacks, add to the juicer (with apple for double the benefits), or boil, steam or roast and serve with main meals. Carrot cake doesn't count.

⊙ Feed a cold, starve a fever

This old wives' tale has been round for centuries. You don't need to do either: it depends whether you are hungry or not—and probably you're not when you have a fever or are coming down with a cold. In both cases, get plenty of rest.

But there may be a grain of truth in it. 'Feed a cold' might work because immune cells that attack viruses are stimulated by food, especially glutamine found in milk, meat and some nuts.

Here's a hot tip. The Cardiff University Common Cold Centre reports that 'any form of hot drink will provide relief from the symptoms of sore throat and cough. The hot fluid has a demulcent and soothing action and tasty drinks containing slightly bitter flavours such as lemon and citric acid are particularly beneficial. Spicy foods and hot soups (chicken included) are also beneficial as they promote airway secretions which have a calmative action on an inflamed throat.'

As for 'starving a fever', as long as you are drinking enough fluids, you should be fine without eating much for a few days (if you have lost your appetite). In fact, having a fever actually increases energy requirements so starving for any length of time is counter-productive but in this case you've probably got bigger problems that need urgent medical attention.

Research
A hot drink may help reduce the symptoms of common colds and flu, according to research by Cardiff University's Common Cold Centre. Researchers have found that a simple hot drink of fruit cordial can provide immediate and sustained relief from

symptoms of runny nose, cough, sneezing, sore throat, chills and tiredness. Published in the December 2008 edition of the clinical journal *Rhinology*, the research compared the effects of a commercially produced apple-and-blackcurrant cordial drink drunk either 'hot' or at room temperature, in 30 volunteers with common cold symptoms. The Centre's director, Professor Ron Eccles, is urging people suffering from colds or flu to have a hot drink to help reduce their symptoms. Professor Eccles said, 'It is surprising that this is the first scientific research on the benefit of a hot drink for treating cold and flu symptoms.'

▶ You need to go to the toilet for number twos every day

Not at all. Everyone's different. It really comes down to how comfortable you feel. If you only go once a week and don't have to strain, that's fine. And if you go several times a day and it doesn't bother you, that's fine, too. 'Normal bowel function ranges from one to two stools (poos) per day to one stool every 3–4 days' according to The Gut Foundation. Constipation, however, is common for people of all ages, especially women. If it's a problem for you, download The Gut Foundation's 'Constipation and Bloating' booklet from the Publications page of their website (www.gutfoundation.com)—it's packed with information including natural remedies.

▶ Spicy foods cause stomach ulcers

No they don't, no matter how much of them you eat or how hot you like your food. Nor does emotional stress. Infection with the *Helicobacter pylori* bacterium is the cause of most peptic ulcers—open sores on the tissue lining of the stomach. Peptic ulcers that occur in the stomach are called gastric ulcers (gastric means stomach). The bugs live in the stomach lining and produce chemicals that cause the irritation and inflammation. We know about this thanks to the truly pioneering work of Nobel laureates Dr Robin Warren and Professor Barry Marshall. Marshall is the man who put his own stomach on the line to prove his point. Back in 1984, he swallowed a brew of cultured *H. pylori*. It gave him ulcer-like symptoms, clearly showing that the bacteria caused ulcers. In the words of the Nobel Committee in 2005, 'Thanks to the pioneering discovery by Marshall and Warren, peptic ulcer disease is no longer a chronic, frequently disabling condition, but a disease that can be cured by a short regimen of antibiotics and acid secretion inhibitors.'

Other causes of stomach ulcers include certain medications taken regularly (eg, aspirin to help prevent heart attack or stroke) and anti-inflammatories (NSAIDS). Stomach cancer can present as an ulcer, especially in older people.

You may want to lay off spicy food if you have an ulcer, but the treatment is antibiotics and drugs to speed the healing process.

⏵ Cloves relieve toothache

Toothache is most often caused by pulpitis—inflammation of the pulp of the tooth—and usually indicates the need for a trip to the dentist pronto for a proper diagnosis and appropriate treatment. It's typically a sign of tooth decay or infection so you don't want to delay.

Dabbing the tooth with a drop of clove oil (not the dried whole flower buds you add to apple pie) has long been a popular home remedy to ease the pain. Pungent clove oil is an essential oil distilled from clove buds (*Syzgium aromaticum*). Its active ingredient, eugenol, has antibacterial and anaesthetic properties. You may find research online suggesting that clove oil can relieve pain as effectively as an anaesthetic gel. However, you have to be careful with 'studies'. It's important to note that the US Food and Drug Administration (FDA) does not believe there is enough evidence to rate eugenol (clove oil) as effective for toothache pain.

So, what to do about that pain in the interim? The best course of action is to ask your dentist when you make the appointment (or your pharmacist if it's the weekend, as it often is when toothache strikes) to suggest suitable pain relief for you until your appointment.

▶ Chewing parsley gets rid of garlic breath

The sulphur compounds that give garlic its fabulous flavour are the culprits behind bad breath that can haunt you (and those around you) for hours—or longer if you have really overdone it.

Chewing a sprig or three of parsley to release breath-freshening oils and mask smelly garlic breath is a remedy that's reputedly been around since Roman times. Why pick parsley? Well, it was plentiful and fresh tasting and we now know it is rich in chlorophyll, a natural breath-freshener commonly added to toothpaste, mouthwash, chewing gum and breath mints.

Parsley may reduce garlic breath, but it doesn't get rid of it. A more effective remedy may be drinking a glass of milk, according to the results of a study published in the *Journal of Food Science*. In tests with raw and cooked garlic cloves, the study authors Dr Sheryl Barringer and Areerat Hansanugrum found that milk 'significantly reduced' levels of the sulphur compounds that give garlic its flavour and pungent smell. Apparently, it is the water and fat in milk that deodorises the breath. Mixing milk with garlic in the mouth before swallowing had a higher odour-neutralising effect than drinking milk after eating the garlic in the trial that scientists performed. And full-fat milk provided better results than skimmed milk or just water, according to breath samples taken from a volunteer. For optimum effect, sip the milk as you eat the garlic, they say.

If this all seems like too much trouble, moderate your garlic eating, choose cooked garlic over raw, or indulge your love of garlic with like-minded family and friends.

⊙ Drink one glass of red wine a day

Taking alcohol for 'medicinal purposes' goes back a long way. Wine has been of interest to nutrition researchers for years because of the so-called 'French paradox'. This term was coined to describe the unexpectedly low rate of coronary heart disease in France, despite the fact that the French are renowned for enjoying foods high in saturated fat, such as butter, cheese, cream, pastry and *paté de foie gras*.

This combination of heart health and high fat piqued the curiosity of researchers who began looking for what else the food-loving French were consuming that might be protecting their hearts. Wine topped their hypothesis list—it is packed with antioxidants (especially red wine) and the French produce and drink a lot of it. A review of scientific studies concluded that daily consumption of 150ml (5fl oz) reduced cardiovascular disease by 32 per cent.

The red versus white wine story is made more complicated by the fact that alcohol itself is thought to reduce the risk of heart disease. Small amounts of anything alcoholic seems to do the trick but I suppose wine is more often enjoyed with meals compared with spirits and beer. It's not what you drink but how that matters.

But lifestyle is important, too. Studies of drinkers in France have shown that those who drink wine in moderation are also less likely to be overweight and more likely to be active and eat a healthy diet overall. Visitors to Paris will notice, for example, that Parisians walk a lot (driving in Paris is a health hazard in itself), almost always take time to enjoy meals, don't snack between meals and eat smaller portions.

So if you do like to drink, limit it to one to two glasses a day because there are health risks involved in drinking alcohol to excess. I have a chapter on alcohol, health, the problem with binge drinking and how to enjoy alcohol in moderation in my book, *Eat to Beat Cholesterol*.

Glossary

ADHD Attention Deficit Hyperactivity Disorder. A behavioural disorder characterised by impulsive behaviour, inattention and hyperactivity.

ALA Alpha-linolenic acid. An essential polyunsaturated fatty acid required in the diet because it cannot be made in the body. Food sources include walnuts, canola oil and flaxseeds.

ALLERGEN A substance that can provoke an allergic reaction in allergic individuals—for example, nut protein can be an allergen in people allergic to nuts.

ALLERGENIC A substance that can be an allergen.

AMYLASE An enzyme that breaks down starch (a type of carbohydrate), found in the saliva and digestive juices.

ANTIOXIDANTS Substances such as phytochemicals and some vitamins found in food that help protect cells by preventing oxidation. They do this by quelling chemical 'free radicals' that can cause damage, and via other mechanisms too such as as reducing inflammation. In food, they are found mostly in plants.

BMR Basal Metabolic Rate. The number of kilojoules (calories) required to maintain basic survival processes in the human body, such as breathing, circulation and metabolism. It does not include the energy needed for physical activity. BMR varies from person to person, depending on age, sex, body size and body composition and represents about 60 to 75 per cent of your metabolic rate.

BIOACCUMULATION The effect of concentrating the levels of a substance (such as a pesticide or heavy metal) within organisms upward through the food chain.

CARBOHYDRATE One of the major nutrients that provide energy in the human diet; includes starches and sugars.

CAROTENOID A type of phytochemical present in richly coloured fruits and vegetables; includes beta-carotene in carrots that converts to vitamin A in the body.

CARCINOGEN A substance that can trigger cancer, either by disruption of normal cellular processes or damaging the DNA.

CARCINOGENIC Describes a substance that has known cancer-triggering effects.

CARIOGENIC The ability to cause dental caries (dental decay).

CORE FOODS Foods that are required in our diet to meet nutritional needs because they contain significant amounts of essential and beneficial nutrients for human health. These are: breads and cereal (grain) foods; vegetables and legumes; fruits; dairy; meat and alternatives. For reasons unknown, healthy fats and oils are also essential and beneficial; however, they are not given core food status.

COELIC DISEASE (OR CELIAC DISEASE) An autoimmune disorder of the small intestine that causes severe and permanent intolerance to gluten, a protein found in commonly eaten grains such as wheat, rye, barley and oats. People with coeliac disease require a gluten-free diet for life.

CLIMATE CHANGE The gradual warming of the atmosphere due to the accumulation of greenhouse gases that prevent heat escaping. Climate change affects temperature, rainfall, wind, sea level, ocean acidity and consequently impacts all human and biological systems on Earth.

CLINICAL TRIAL A type of scientific biomedical or health experiment conducted in controlled conditions according to predetermined protocol. Typically, a group of people is subjected to a change, called an intervention or treatment, and compared with another group that has not received the treatment (called the control group) in order to assess the effect of the treatment.

DENTAL CARIES Tooth decay. Plaque bacteria on the tooth surface utilise sugars and starches in food and produce acid, which can form cavities (holes) in enamel coating. If left untreated cavities can cause tooth abscess and loss of the tooth.

DHA Docosahexanoic Acid. One of three essential long-chain omega-3 polyunsaturated fats found in the human diet, mostly in fish and seafood but also in lean red meat and eggs. Important for heart and brain health.

DIABETES A condition in which the body is unable to properly control the level of glucose in the blood because it no longer produces the hormone insulin (type 1 diabetes), or the insulin does not work effectively (type 2 diabetes).

DIETITIAN A university-trained health professional specialising in optimising food and nutrition for health and the management of disease for both individuals and groups. Appropriately trained and regulated practitioners can be found via national accreditation bodies. Accredited Practising Dietitian, APD (Australia); Registered Dietitian, RD (USA, UK, New Zealand and Canada).

EPIDEMIOLOGICAL STUDY (OR POPULATION STUDY) A type of study on a group (defined by age, gender, occupation or location, etc) or population to identify and describe health, disease and environmental characteristics to determine risk or protective factors.

EPA Eicosapentanoic acid. An essential long-chain omega-3 fat important for heart and brain health. Best dietary sources are fish and seafood.

EPA Environmental Protection Authority (Australian state and territories); Environmental Protection Agency (USA). Government authority responsible for protecting health and the environment.

FDA Food and Drug Administration. US government agency within the Department of Health and Human Services with responsibility for protecting public health by assuring the safety of food, medicines, medical equipment and personal care products, as well as reducing the use of tobacco.

FRUITARIAN A person claiming to exist on a diet of fruit and little else.

FLAVONOIDS A large family of antioxidants in plant foods and drinks. Examples include anthocyanins in berries; flavanols in tea, apples, red wine and chocolate; and flavanones in citrus fruits.

Food allergy A condition in which a person's immune system is triggered by consuming allergens in food (eg, milk, nuts or eggs), causing an allergic reaction. People with food allergy must totally avoid the food allergen.

Food intolerance (or food chemical sensitivity) Sensitivity to natural or added chemicals in food (eg, lactose, glutamates) that cause a variety of unpleasant but not serious symptoms. Symptoms can usually be controlled by reducing the amount of the problematic food chemical(s) in the diet rather than total avoidance.

Glycemic index A ranking of the effect of carbohydrate-containing foods on blood glucose levels. High GI foods cause blood glucose level to rise to high levels quickly; low GI foods have lesser effect on blood glucose levels.

GM food Genetically modified food. Foods derived from crops that have been genetically manipulated to have desired characteristics (eg, pesticide resistance).

Goitre Swelling of the thyroid gland in the neck, most commonly caused by a deficiency of iodine in the diet.

Goitrogen Substances that inhibit uptake of iodine by the thyroid gland, which may then cause goitre. Mild goitrogens exist in some raw plant foods, but are not known to cause problems in healthy people.

Greenhouse Gas (GHG) Gases, mainly carbon dioxide, methane, nitrous oxide and synthetic fluorinated gases, that trap heat from the sun in the atmosphere and thereby contribute to climate change.

Heavy metal One of a group of elements that have metallic properties; they can be either natural or man-made. Some are toxic— (eg, mercury, lead, plutonium).

Homogenisation The process of breaking large cream droplets in milk into smaller ones under very high pressure. It gives milk an even, creamy texture without a cream layer on top.

Hormonal Growth Promotants (HGPs) HGPs improve the efficiency by which cattle convert stockfeed into meat and contain naturally occurring hormones (oestrogen, progesterone and testosterone) or synthetic hormones (trenbolone acetate or zeranol).

Insulin Hormone secreted by the pancreas that regulates blood glucose levels and helps glucose to enter cells to produce energy. It also prevents fat being used for energy. People with type 1 diabetes produce no insulin and require insulin injections. In type 2 diabetes, insulin doesn't work effectively and this is called insulin resistance.

Insulin resistance (IR) A condition in which insulin doesn't work properly, resulting in high blood glucose levels. Insulin resistance occurs in the metabolic syndrome, obesity, type 2 diabetes and pre-diabetes, and also increases the risk of cardiovascular disease.

Kilojoule 1000 joules. The joule is the globally accepted modern unit of measurement of the energy contained in food, as per the International System of Units (abbreviated to SI for the French Systeme International d'unites). The old metric unit—the calorie—is still used in some countries, including the USA.

LIPOGENESIS The formation of body fat (also called adipogenesis).

LONG-CHAIN OMEGA-3 FATS Essential polyunsaturated fats (fatty acids) needed in the diet and important for heart and brain health: DHA (Docosohexanoic Acid) and EPA (Eicosopentanoic Acid). Found in fish, seafood, lean red meat and eggs (and fish oil supplements).

LOW GI DIET A diet including lower GI carbohydrate foods, which provokes a lower blood glucose response. Low GI diets have health benefits for everyone, but especially those with diabetes or pre-diabetes.

MACRONUTRIENTS Nutrients that are needed in large amounts (eg, protein) compared with micronutrients that are needed in tiny amounts (eg, vitamin C). Macronutrients are water, carbohydrates, proteins, fats and alcohol. Alcohol is a non-essential nutrient.

MACULAR DEGENERATION (OR AGE-RELATED MACULAR DEGENERATION OR AMD) Eye disease in which the centre of the retina (the macular) deteriorates, causing poor vision. The risk of AMD increases with age.

METABOLIC RATE How many kilojoules we require each day: consists of Basal Metabolic Rate (BMR); thermic effect of food (or thermogenesis); and energy required for physical activity.

METABOLIC SYNDROME A simultaneous combination of conditions that increases the risk of cardiovascular disease and diabetes: a large waist (central obesity); high blood triglyceride level; high blood pressure; low HDL (good) cholesterol; and high blood glucose (blood sugar) level.

METHODOLOGY The way a scientific study is planned and conducted: design, sampling, data collection, data analysis.

METHODOLOGICAL Pertaining to the methodology of a scientific study. Studies can be criticised on methodological grounds if they use inappropriate methodology, or if appropriate methodology is used poorly and therefore the results could be misleading.

MICRONUTRIENTS Nutrients needed in tiny amounts: vitamins, minerals, trace elements.

MRL Maximum residue limit. The highest permitted level of a pesticide residue in a food not expected to cause harm to human health. These are set and regulated by countries/regions—for example, the USDA (the USA), EU (European Union) and FSANZ (Australia and New Zealand).

NUTRIGENETICS Personalised diets designed to suit an individual's genetic make up.

NUTRITIONIST Can be an alternate title for university-trained dietitian but not always. Anyone can call themselves a nutritionist because the term is not regulated in most countries. People who have studied nutrition or nutrition science but who have not done the necessary clinical training to prescribe dietary therapy call themselves nutritionists, as do complementary health practitioners like naturopaths.

NSAIDS Non-steroidal Anti-inflammatory Drugs—for example, aspirin, ibuprofen, naproxen.

OBESOGENIC An environment that promotes weight gain. Affluent countries such as the UK, USA, New Zealand and Australia are considered obesogenic for such reasons as energy-dense food is easily available and sold in large portions and there are few opportunities for physical activity.

OMNIVOROUS Eating a mixed diet, including animal and plant foods.

PHENOLIC Describes the presence of natural phenols and polyphenols found in plant foods.

PHYTOCHEMICALS (OR PHYTONUTRIENTS) Naturally occurring substances in plants—including antioxidants, flavonoids, phenolic acids and carotenoids—that have a variety of beneficial properties.

PHYTOESTROGEN A type of polyphenol phytochemical with very weak hormonal effects; includes isoflavones and coumestans. Most commonly found in soy beans and red clover.

POLYMORPHISM Natural variation in particular genes; can convey differences in susceptibility to disease.

POLYPHENOLS A class of beneficial antioxidant found in foods, such as vegetables, legumes, fruit, tea, chocolate and honey.

SATIETY The state of fullness or satisfaction after eating; absence of hunger.

STARCH A type of carbohydrate consisting of a chain or matrix of sugar molecules; (amylase or amylopectin). Found in grains and flour, legumes and starchy vegetables.

TEFLON A brand of industrial fluoropolymer coating made by DuPont used on non-stick cookware.

THERMOGENESIS (OR THERMIC EFFECT OF FOOD) The amount of energy used to digest and process food. It is a small part of the energy (kilojoules/calories) we require each day (see Metabolic rate).

USDA United States Department of Agriculture.

VEGAN A person who eats no animal foods (including dairy), a total vegetarian.

Acknowledgements

I am eternally grateful to Philippa Sandall for her contributions to this book and her ongoing support, encouragement and faith in me and my writing. I would also like to thank Fiona Shultz from New Holland for her belief in the whole idea and Mary Trewby for her deft editing. And thank you to colleagues near and far for your support, especially during the backlash I sometimes get when sticking my neck out for the nutritional truth. And of course thanks are due to my husband, family and friends who help me feel none of it matters anyway!

Index

About the author

Nicole Senior is an accredited practising dietitian and nutritionist who loves writing and talking about food and health. She is known for her straight-talking, common-sense approach that helps make healthy eating simple and achievable for everyone. Nicole is a food lover with a passion for turning complex nutrition science into simple everyday eating advice. Nicole's previous books are *Eat to Beat Cholesterol*, *Heart Food*, and *Belly Busting for Blokes*.

Also from New Holland Publishers:

Nicole Senior & Veronica Cuskelly

BELLY BUSTING
FOR BLOKES

5 STEPS TO
BUST THE BULGE

Reduce your waist, improve your life—how to eat and move your way to health

ISBN 9781742571492

Eat to beat
cholesterol

- how to lower your cholesterol level
- eating plans to suit your lifestyle
- over 100 recipes
- shopping and cooking tips

Nicole Senior APD & Veronica Cuskelly

ISBN 9781741104493

First published in 2012 by
New Holland Publishers (Australia) Pty Ltd
Sydney • Auckland • London • Cape Town
www.newholland.co.au

1/66 Gibbes Street Chatswood NSW 2067 Australia
218 Lake Road Northcote Auckland New Zealand
86 Edgware Road LondonW2 2EA United Kingdom
80 McKenzie Street Cape Town 8001 South Africa

A record of this book is available at the National Library of Australia

ISBN: 9781742571485

Although every effort has been made to ensure the contents of this book are accurate
at the time of printing, it must not be treated as a substitute for qualified medical
advice. Always consult a qualified medical practitioner. Neither the author or the
publisher can be held responsible for any loss or claim arising out of the use or misuse
of the suggestions, or failure to take medical care.

Publisher: Fiona Schultz
Publishing manager: Lliane Clarke
Senior editor: Mary Trewby
Proofreader: Catherine Etteridge
Cover designer: Celeste Vlok
Designer: Kimberley Pearce
Production manager: Olga Dementiev
Printer: Toppan Leefung Printing Limited

10 9 8 7 6 5 4 3 2 1

Follow New Holland Publishers on
Facebook: www.facebook.com/NewHollandPublishers and Twitter: @
NewHollandAU